Ginger and Ganesh

Ginger and Ganesh

Adventures in Indian Cooking, Culture and Love

NANI POWER

COUNTERPOINT

BERKELEY

Library of Congress Cataloging-in-Publication Data:

Power, Nani.
Ginger and Ganesh : adventures in Indian cooking, culture, and love / by Nani Power.
p. cm.
ISBN 978-1-58243-544-2
1. Cookery, Indic. I. Title.

TX724.5.I4P67 2010
641.5954—dc22

2009052552

Cover design by Ann Weinstock
Interior design by Megan Jones Design

Printed in the United States of America

COUNTERPOINT
2117 Fourth Street
Suite D
Berkeley, CA 94710

www.counterpointpress.com

Distributed by Publishers Group West

10 9 8 7 6 5 4 3 2 1

O elephant-faced God, Ganesha,
you are served by the attendants of Shiva
and you eat forest apples and blackberries.
You are Uma's son, the destroyer of sorrows.
I bow to the lotus feet of the remover of obstacles.

CONTENTS

The Ad

Please Teach Me Indian Vegetarian Cooking! (Northern Va)

I will bring ingredients and pay you $10/hr for your trouble.
I would like to know about your culture as well.

*I*N A SIMPLE desire to learn Indian cooking hands-on, I placed this ad on Craigslist not knowing how much it would change my life. I wanted to cook real Indian food. I didn't want the sterile environment of a restaurant or the studied air of a professional teacher. I craved the person-to-person teaching of yesteryear amidst the homeyness of a real kitchen. I wanted to learn the art of curries and chutneys through the senses, not just through the measuring and timing of a cold cookbook.

You see, I'm not really American, at least in terms of my palate. I seem to be hard-wired with South Asian taste buds, a person that craves the burn of chilies and mustard seed, the warm heat of ginger, cumin, and cinnamon, and the bitterness of asafetida and black salt. I don't know why. I have been like this as long as I can remember.

I go to barbecues, picnics, and dinner parties inwardly yawning. I crave the waft of a fresh masala, the stain of turmeric far beyond the yellow hue it offers French's mustard.

So what did I—spice craver, born in the land of bland food—do before this, during the first part of my life in the casserole-laden, fondue-fixing '60s? What any reasonable person does: I bought cookbooks and studied them. I ground stale supermarket cumin seeds and cinnamon sticks, sizzled spice after spice, a lone voyager for flavor. I wrestled with samosa dough, and ended up eating a lot of watery, soulless curries and stone-hard samosas. Sigh. Went to restaurants and visited the steam buffets consisting of endless anonymous brown mixtures. I was somewhat satisfied (it was better than a burger) and yet, I felt there was something missing. My palate seemed to insist it was so.

So many things in my life seem to follow this pattern—the search for love and my vocation, as well. A person exists in a semi-pleased daze of unrecognition, colorless, for the blind do not know colors. Then, there comes the fateful day when you are awakened and color bursts in.

Fast forward to now: I am a single woman in my forties who uses Craigslist for most everything—buying an entertainment center or sofa, meeting up with fellow salsa dancers, advertising writing classes. One desperate Friday evening I bought cheap eyelash extensions from a young Korean beauty student, and a rather bad haircut as well. Once, I traded a homemade apple pie with an electrician for installing dimmers in my house. His wife, who was eight months pregnant, was too tired to bake. They came as a couple to my house, where I greeted them with the wafting smells of sweet apples and cinnamon. The wife, young and Filipino, sat and chatted with me, while her husband, an American in a large Redskins jersey, pulled out his tools. But one day, while eating another tepid version of Aloo Gobi, I finally had a brainstorm and placed the ad.

TO MY COMPLETE shock, my email account was instantly flooded with responses from every age and from every region. Wading through them—they ranged from perfect English to unintelligible, from polite to sharp—I managed to set up a few appointments. They would supply the ingredients and I would just show up. I was so excited, and still am, every time I stand on the front stoop, listening to the soft rustling of a stranger unlocking the door. It is somehow both a great mystery and a profound gift, to be able to enter someone's house for food. One surprising thing I found, entering these houses, leaving my shoes at the door, roasting spices with strangers, laughing, tasting, and sharing their lives, was that much more than cooking occurred. A certain antique rite, a female coming-of-age, so to speak, was being reenacted. I was learning to cook in the most ancient of ways—woman to woman, with all the senses and a great deal of warmth. I was welcomed like a family member, and taught in the same patient and loving ways their own mothers had guided them through the years.

This book is about the masala of my own life—my journey resembled the separate spices of who I am transforming into an intricate blend. I will take the reader through the doorways of these women, where we lovingly cooked together and bonded in our cultures. The recipes are not your typical Indian curry take-out. These are treasured family recipes from vegetarian homes in India—from Shahi Paneer, a dish of homemade cheese cubes in a rich tomato and cashew curry, to coconut-stuffed okra, to luscious potato-curry dumplings.

These recipes will be a welcome addition to any Indian aficionado's repertoire, as well as a temptation for the average cook seeking to expand his or her roster of healthy vegetarian foods. They are the well-known comfort foods of any vegetarian home in India. Ask an Indian about Pau Bhaji, found on Mumbai's Chowpatty beach, or the rich, dark chickpea stew with fried bhaure bread called Chole Bhature, famous in the Punjab, and you'll see a visceral look of desperate homesickness and drool. These foods are the staples of longing and memory. They are dishes you will make again and again.

Almost imperceptibly, the culture of this rich and varied country slithered into my life like a sinuous cobra, combining the modern ways of the United States with the Technicolor of India, while I ate some damn good food. I wanted to understand the Indian culture and people; and what seemed so enchanting was that I was constantly being surprised and challenged by how complex—and contradictory—it can be. While at one time thousands of years old, in another time it seems jauntily modern, yet where this occurs bewilders me. I have learned to keep an open mind. Now, after this year of cooking real Indian food, I realize that the only real way to learn to cook is through the senses and heart. It turns out that it is the only real way to live and to love, as well.

LET ME TELL you about myself first. I am a completely untraditional, divorced single mother with two kids; a writer of novels, living hand-to-mouth, essentially, and yet striving to live a life of meaning and substance. I am also a great cook, or so "they" say. Actually, before I became a writer, I eked out a living as a caterer and still occasionally will do so, between books. After a long day of writing, nothing is more therapeutic for me than cooking. On a weekend, I am one of those urban trekkers who loves scouting around and digging through tiny foreign grocers for odd herbs, incense, unusual vegetables. In some sense, it satisfies my wanderlust in a cheap way—a quick afternoon journey to Thailand or Guatemala through the stalls of a shop. And on another level, this habit—albeit temporarily—seems to quell my voracious appetite for sensual adventure, so glaringly absent in these beige plastic clusters of suburbia where I live.

I am a new growing species in these states—a Disenchanted, Educated, Single, Boomer, Yearning. Indians call themselves *Desis* (from a Sanskrit word meaning "from the country"), so I call women like me *DESBYs*—Wanna-Be Desis. We crave the pageantry, tradition, history, connection, and spirituality of India, yet with our independent, willful, overeducated backgrounds, we would no doubt explode if seriously involved in such a duty-oriented society. We prefer to do yoga, meditate, wear a sari, eat dal, and play the role. Indians laugh at our childlike behavior, but it is actually no laughing matter. Just like the popular Indian-used term ABCD (American Born Confused Desi), we Desbys are stuck in between worlds, seeking balance and continuity, while our attention spans are pretty short and we are very accustomed to our freedom.

I find now after this yearlong cooking frenzy, this spice journey, that I am a changed person because I was allowed into a sacred circle, into the private center of a family's home—the kitchen. I was treated like a guest, a family member, and a friend eating their food. Being part of their life, chitchatting with a steaming mug of chai, made me reexamine things in my life beyond food, concepts that had been unhinged for sometime, floating amorphously in a stew of indecision and curiosity: love, spirituality, femininity.

This simple yearlong cooking lesson—innocently started as a little two-line ad on Craigslist because I was frustrated with my lame attempts at Palak Paneer—taught me a lot more than how to make a killer spinach and cheese curry. It smashed open my heart, in so many ways. The kindness of the women, the beauty of the culture, the explosion of flavors, and, curiously, the very physical act of cooking led me to examine what is beyond all this: the spiritual realm.

ON THIS PATH I met Sri Ganesh. You may be familiar with him: he is the ever-popular elephant-headed deity, accompanied by a tiny mouse. He has a large jovial belly, and holds a conch shell. I'm not sure why he in particular ignited my passion for this culture and beyond, but perhaps it was the fact that his statue was present the first time I tasted the incendiary potions of India I came to love. Or maybe, the wisdom and calm that he emanates soothed my world-weary soul, and he seemed to be a constant reminder—at the doorway of most houses, or in their altars—that I was on a spiritual path as well as physical. Thus, not only was this a quest for ginger, the taste of India, but also a search for the essence of this wonderful avatar loved by so many. I explore in these pages, for example, the many ways Ganesh, familiar to some, exotic to others, inhabits a vital part of the houses I visit and how I attempt to pay tribute to him on my own. Offerings to Ganesh are expected at any creative venture, and as I write this book, I find my relationship with this deity beginning. I am not a Hindu or particularly a Christian, preferring to call myself a seeker, yet Ganesh touched my heart.

This book of spices is more than a journey into the female psyche through the sensuality of our palates. It is a journey of my own personal trials, seeking solace, love, and connection in this world I live in. Unexpectedly along the way, tasting exotic curries in stranger's homes, I found more than just cooking on Craigslist: I found love, in the most unexpected way: a man, from India, too young for comfort, too handsome for words, difficult and tempestuous, kind and giving.

More than anything, this is a journey into myself, but it is also about all modern American women—all Desbys—living in this country, who find themselves divorced, alone, seeking. We are women who struggle to identify where the feminine lies. Somehow cooking resonates with that search. Even though men dominate the professional world of cooking, the home and hearth have been traditionally ruled by the woman. American women have come so far in our independence and freedom, and yet I feel, given the popularity of Martha Stewart, The Food Network, and cooking classes nationwide, we need to reclaim this territory again, in our own terms. We need to understand this nurturing side of ourselves without the classic shackles that it once represented.

THIS STORY HAS only begun.

As I finish this book, my next journey is India herself.

But in the meantime, this book is an examination of my yearlong saga of love and spices, found on Craigslist. And what is more modern than that? Years back we had to take an airplane or boat to connect with another culture. These days, we need only have computer access.

And the responses flood my email and I am always packing up to enter another house, perched in the suburbs; to open a strange door, eyes smarting from the rush of the hot steam of roasted chilies; and to find a new friend.

Another response just came from my ad, from a woman named Padma. I am quite eager to get to know her. I send her this email:

Dear Padma—

Yes, My name is Nani and I am interested. Where are you from and what do you like to cook?

Thanks—

Nani

I don't hear back from her for a couple of days. And then, this:

Hi Nani,

My husband doesn't want me to pursue this. There goes one of the lessons in Indian culture.

Padma

And thus ends the story of Padma, so brief, and yet so illuminating.

I read it with curiosity. I have no husband to tell me what to do. Nor do I have a husband to care about what I do. Wistfulness ensues, yet with confusion. The Desby dilemma.

Read on, and let's eat some good food.

Waiting for Ganesh

A girl looks for spices. A woman finds them,
and meets an Elephant God

I'VE BEEN PASSIONATELY in love with Indian cooking for thirty
years—ever since I was in my teens and an older gentleman, a
friend of the family, a world raconteur, took me to Georgetown
to a white tablecloth affair in a raj-like atmosphere, with sitar-playing
musicians and turbaned waiters. Of course, I was enchanted by this,
but it was the arrival of a swamp-green bowl of coriander chutney that
blew me away (back then, in the '70s, we called it "coriander," which
of course I had never seen as this was the pre-cilantro era). Oh, try this,
said my friend who had been many times to India. The spicy yet soapy
taste intoxicated and mystified me. I was hooked. A large elephant-
headed deity stood at the doorway, festooned with flowers, sprinkled
with turmeric, surrounded by burning incense. What is that? I asked
innocently.

That, my friend said, is Lord Ganesh. You don't know Ganesh?

I was eighteen. No, I didn't know Ganesh. I knew a small, stone
Episcopal Church in my tiny town of Delaplane, Virginia, that had a
large simple brass cross on the altar, where we attended after my mother
remarried. I knew my deeply Catholic grandfather on my father's side
and the velvet-cloaked altar in his house, with a carved crucifix inside

of Jesus in thorns. I knew a golden Buddha my mother kept in a small altar in our house, with a flower tucked inside, being the daughter in a foreign service family and having lived for years in Thailand. All these cross-cultural connections led to a mishmash of thoughts, but no clear direction. But this? His wise-appearing eyes shone out. He had the body of a man, with a large stomach. It was sensual, and assaulting—half man, half elephant, yet strangely comforting.

Thank him, my friend suggested.

I did.

He is the remover of obstacles, he said. Very important.

I FORGOT ABOUT Ganesh for some time, but not about Indian food: a suburban foray into the strip malls of Virginia found Indian Spices and Appliances, where I stocked up on all sorts of cookbooks (usually self-published paperbacks with bad, blurry color reproductions, written by Mrs. So-and-So), jumbo bags of spices (apparently one couldn't buy simply a small jar of turmeric, one had to buy a crate of the stuff, which lasts forever), and various implements, of which I knew not how to use. Compare this to the spice department in your local grocery store: tiny jars containing a few tablespoons of curry powder, usually old and stale, selling for exorbitant prices.

During this time, I studied cookbooks and tried to re-create the dark, fairly unctuous-tasting, mysterious stews I found in Indian restaurants. I hadn't tried Indian home-cooking—I thought what I was eating in restaurants was the norm. Little did I know!

I puttered around for years, trying all forms of vindaloos, curries, puffs, chutneys, but nothing tasted really good. My curries were watery, full of raw spice. My chutneys, overly gingered or bland. But a quest for wondrous food by reading cookbooks only goes so far: life is an experiential teacher. I remembered the smell of the incense and the statue of

Ganesh: as a young woman, I was deeply attracted to the idea of God and spirituality, yet I had been subjected only to church, which I found insufferably boring, tedious, fake, and worst of all, it always smelled bad. I realize now the aura of ritual was missing, which even at my young age, spoke little of joy or ceremony. Hymns seemed heavy and ponderous to me. Still, I sensed that truth lay in all the religious texts, so I read them, anything I could get my hands on. I found the true teachings of Christ beautiful, love-filled, and thoughtful—I just didn't like the vehicle. For years, I attended a Unitarian church in New York to get my spiritual fix, but found it had the same pared down lack of wonder as the others.

I went to Brazil and was intrigued by the Candomblé rituals I saw on the beaches, where followers left burning candles. One walked out the door at a fashionable restaurant at the heavily trafficked crossroads in Ipanema, only to almost walk into sacrificed chickens. Walking on the beach late one night, I witnessed such a ritual. A woman was possessed by Oxum, Goddess of love, beauty, fertility, and wealth. As the others drummed, the woman danced in a frenzy, laughing around a fire built on the sand. She cackled and sang. And then she saw me, and came forward, a jar of honey in her hand, enticing me to eat it, as she scooped up a spoonful. I was about to go to her—I was enchanted—when I was stopped by a harsh *No* from the priest, who pulled her away. You are not ready for this, he said. Of course not, I was in formation. My friends explained that I hadn't been protected, that I needed to know the essence of the Candomblé to accept the gift, that it could be dangerous to my spirit. Nevertheless, it probably was dangerous to my spirit anyway: it left me hungry and searching for more. The thought that somewhere, beyond these soft and gentle suburban hills, there existed something alive and pulsing: in the food, in the rituals. Be it Brazil or Africa, Costa Rica or Nepal, it existed. And India seemed to call to me personally.

Jump ahead fifteen years: I am married, pregnant, have a three-year-old son, and live in Brooklyn. Fortunately my son has an Indian playmate, a son of two doctors, and the two boys and his nanny and I hang out together, a woman from Kerala, in Southern India. Lo and behold, I am swept away again—entranced by the southern delights of idli cakes and dosas, coconut chutneys and curry leaves. Stella kindly teaches me a few dishes—which become cupboard standards for me. This is my first time encountering real home-cooked dal, which tastes like heaven, flecked with mustard seeds and curry leaves, as is the southern tradition, as opposed to the mud-like porridge generally served in restaurants. Finally, I know what my taste buds have been craving all these years.

We moved away from Brooklyn, after my few months of initiation into the rites of dal and dosas, and years passed by, with nary an Indian flavor, save an occasional buffet here and there or frozen samosas. A divorce followed and a long period of adjustment. Much food was cooked between catering and feeding my sons, heralding the holidays or just simple, comfort fare, but very few Indian dishes passed through our kitchen. No one seemed to share my passion, especially my two little boys who only wanted the simplest nibbles. But after some time, the lion of my spice cravings reared its head once more and I took charge, eschewing the books this time.

It hit me. Why couldn't I learn from another Stella? Where was Stella? (I never found her again. She went back to India.) In desperation, I put out the ad. It was almost like I was searching for connection as well as good food. Who would've guessed that I would find culture, as well? Or even love? Yes, not only was my appetite for real Indian food reawakened in the home kitchens of my Indian neighbors, but my heart was reawakened—after a long, cold spell after divorce—by a love affair with a man who hails from India. Through the process of cooking in these homes, I also found a new spiritual partner, someone I'll call "V," a man I could discuss all my interests with, without deities or dogma, an exploration of the consciousness of one's self. I went looking for Ginger and I found Ganesh. The musings of my palate led me to the cravings of my heart.

I see a small statue of Ganesh in an Indian store, staring at me with his doleful eyes.

I buy it. I buy incense. I start thanking him and ask him to clear obstacles, to bless my creativity. I read Ganesh likes bananas and I give him one occasionally.

Slowly, the obstacles fell away on this journey, and the doors flew open, leading me into a path of discovery, love, and coconut chutney.

Vishnu of Suburbia

The teeming bazaar of the market is now a cold, plastic Costco.
But you can still buy basmati rice in a burlap sack

So, OFF TO the suburbs in search of real Indian food and perhaps more (adventures!), I drive into the gleaming developments, with their spraying fake lakes, the hot sun beaming on the sticky asphalt. Houses neatly packed in streets with cleverly wrought names—Mooncourt, Fieldstream—as somehow poetic tidbits meant to evoke a new world.

It is a new world.

Technology companies line Route 50 and the surrounding areas. BMWs shine in the parking lots, lovingly washed by their owners, and, looking around one would think they had strayed into some expensive gated community in India. Everyone is Indian. They wear the popular sporty clothes of Nike and Adidas, they drive American gas-guzzlers, and they fill their carts at Costco with Go-Gurts and frozen Mystic pizzas like any American soccer mom.

But when I enter the homes, my shoes left at the door, it is as if stepping back through the centuries. Gone is the flash of modern American culture. Breads are made by hand, quickly squeezed and rolled on round wooden blocks, and seared on old cast iron tawas (flat griddles). And the spices they use have been used for thousands of years, each with medicinal purposes, each lending a subtle note to the finished dish.

These methods have survived in a world spinning as fast as we can stand, hurtling us forward into ever-fresher horizons. And yet, behind the doors the ancient world still exists: women passing on their treasured dishes to each other. No, you roll like this. Here, try like this one. Our throats slightly choking as hot chili oils fill the air. The delicate and mysterious paste of sweets brought over on the plane from Gujarat, most generously offered. It's an ancient bonding and one I seem to need, the feminine tradition of hearth-tending. Why have we fallen away from it in our rush to succeed in the world? Why is cooking a lovingly prepared meal from natural ingredients, from "scratch" as we like to say, gone to the wayside? And, as a vegetarian, flexitarian, or even plain meat-eater, who wouldn't want to learn the vast bevy of vegetable dishes that Indians delight in?

There is another element at play in this journey: my newfound vegetarianism comes from a place where I am trying to experience *ahimsa*, the Hindu and Buddhist concept of "do no harm." Of course, this applies to what we consume; essentially, animals that have experienced harm and violence arrive on our dinner plates. But I am also exploring the idea that energy, positive or negative, can permeate our food. We talk of food "cooked with love" as if it palpably makes a difference to our taste buds, and I think it does. Surely the energetic state of food preparation—either in a cold, sterile factory or the hands of a loving person—contributes to the blandness or the goodness and delectability of food. I have to believe this is so, even for those who would mock such new age thinking. Therefore, it seems to me that when we are taught cooking, person to person, we are engaged in the highest method of teaching, a shared respect and kindness, a cultural exchange and a lasting warmth that just reading a recipe cannot impart. Well, you may say, isn't that what you are producing here, just another book? Yes, but I am hoping that these recipes feel as authentic and true as when they emerge from the hands and mouths of these ladies, and that you too will feel the love and kindness that was imparted. These weren't produced in test kitchens: they were shared like old stories, lovingly described and respected. And I am hoping that this will encourage you to reach out to your neighbors, be they from Pakistan or Romania or Appalachia or Long Island, and ask them: What are your family recipes? Can you teach me?

I notice a stark difference culturally in kitchens between Indian and American concepts: Americans have transformed their cooking spaces, or at least they long to, into casual centers of social entertaining—islands with stools for lounging on with chardonnay as the host chops a few shallots. Americans have great grills for flaming this and that. Even a sitting area bleeding into the area for more social activity. And, if you can afford state of the art technology for the best culinary experience, customized sub zero refrigerators. There are Aga stoves that keep temperature perfect for instant baking, pizza ovens, wine coolers, etc. And yet, in these kitchens, most do not cook. Bring them a chicken and they will look at it warily. Show them a pile of okra and they will not know what to do. Cooking has come to mean an entirely different thing: there is so much convenient food, cooking has been stripped of its sensuality. We do not need to touch food to make a meal. We are opening packages. Salad and vegetables are packaged, as well as meat. We tear these open, slide them on a plate. Dinner is done without a hand actually touching it.

The Indian kitchen is simple, a factory with a few well-worn tools: cutting board, knife, pressure cooker, chapathi roller, tawa, and blender. Besides a few pans and such, that is it. Oh, and a precious spice tin that they all seem to have: a cylindrical container with six spice bowls and a small spoon, kept by the stove, called a masala dabba.

AND SO, ON my strange modern journey of female apprenticeship, I drive through the plasticized furrows of Virginia, venturing into a smooth and expressionless development to augur the elements of an ancient rite: cooking and talking with women who will teach me the methods of a home. In a sense it is like sitting in the darkness of a cool movie theater, awaiting the feature. I am expectant and happy. There is a great sense of trust already flowing through the air, because first of all, the domestic location has eased everyone's minds. It feels safe and comfy. And next, there is a certain respect being shared and honored, that I, coming from such a modern country, would care to know these things. Most of the people who responded to my ad seemed genuinely surprised that I cared to know about their food. But where else would I learn? From a cold book procured at Borders, flopping on my table, as I try to measure the ingredients? How would this teach me anything? I was craving continuity, connection. A femaleness. This is how we do it. And it's complicated, Indian food. There are many spices and herbs, added at specific times. Of course, I would come to realize that everyone, naturally, had their own ways and methods, and that in navigating this journey I would find my own way. Which is a microcosm of life anyway.

MY FIRST HOUSE, a woman named Mishti. I am almost there . . .

I start to wonder, with a small nudging of pain: I'm looking for cooking lessons. Or am I? Am I looking for a mother? a friend? or an artificial lever into another's culture? These thoughts pervade as I career through the trimmed suburbs. I wish to learn but not intrude. I try and keep that in mind.

Meanwhile, I am lost in a maze of beige houses made of siding and fake rock. I turn around and start again. They all look the same.

I look at my address again. Yes, back the other way.

I turn around.

I have come to my first house, first cooking lesson and I am walking up to the door.

My first encounter—the sharp, bracing tang of ginger.

LIKE I SAID, here I am: in my forties, divorced, with two kids. I live in Virginia solely for the sake of my kids. My family is nearby and very present in our lives. It is exurbia, rural countryside of horse farms bleeding into the new sterile suburbs. There are certain reasons that I prefer this to a homey old cabin on a farm: upkeep. I can't deal with furnaces and leaky windows, lawns to trim and hedges to clip. I come and go and write, and that is all I can do. I can also cook. But I fit in very few categories. I am not the barbecuing, SUV-driving suburban mom surrounding me. I am single, and therefore on some level cast out of this group. I don't merge with the immigrant families, such as my Indian neighbors: they keep to themselves. Am I searching for a husband? No. I am happy to live my own life. Am I searching for love? Of course. But what am I not searching for? I am always essentially in the mode of *searching*. On any given day I could choose to eat from twenty-two different regional foods, from Vietnamese to Ethiopian. I can date men from the local country fields or go to Washington DC and dance with politicians, or meet an Egyptian waiter or a Russian mathematician. I can go online and meet Turkish men or African or Arab. I could go live in Nepal or move to New York City. I have too many choices. I am *too* free on some levels. So I come back to basics. Love. Friendship. Cooking.

This act of searching led me to Craigslist, to a community of ladies, of all ages, all classes, from various regions spanning the great continent of India all nestled in the suburbs, who were willing to teach me the vegetarian foods of their great country.

And then, via Craigslist, I also fell in love. Searching isn't a bad thing. Sometimes you can find what you are searching for.

Krishna and Curry Leaves

Miracles abound

*I*T IS SUMMER of 2008. I am driving towards my first cooking class, a bag of vegetables beside me, as given to me on a list in the email.

I am tired. I just got back from vacation with my kids and my then-boyfriend. We had been together for two years and had become engaged. But the vacation seemed to break open the deep incongruities in our relationship, and the fissures widened. We fought and didn't talk. We came back and it was all over.

On some level, I have to examine the fact that I felt I needed this relationship—that he had two boys like myself, and that I needed to remarry and have a stable home environment. But did I really love him, did he inspire me, was he someone I loved to talk to at the end of the day? Not really. We actually had nothing in common.

But then one starts to think: I have lived the family life with child rearing. What am I seeking exactly? I started to consider something more. I spent hours debating this with friends. It was an open dialogue, one that was not meant to be solved as much as discussed, endlessly. Soul mate vs. simple companion vs. friend with benefits vs. sugar daddy vs. best buddy—we jumped around with so many theories and ideas, if we were seeking the cure for cancer we probably already would have

the Nobel in our hands. But of course, with all this talk, we had nothing and knew nothing. Just a liberal bunch of women dancing salsa or
zydeco, going to farmers' markets, attending yoga ashrams, drinking
pinot grigio and trying out Buddhism. Dating here and there, with not
much enthusiasm.

But I did know one thing. I wanted to learn Indian food. I didn't
think these two things, however, had much to do with each other. I was
wrong.

MY FIRST TEACHER said she was from Gujarat, the most northwestern
state in India. A quick bit of Googling and I discovered that the people
are known for their sharp business sense. In fact, out of Forbes's list of
the ten richest men in India, four of them are Gujarati. Gandhi was also
"guju," as slang would put it. They also house the most vegetarians in
all of India, and as every Indian will tell me in the days to come:

Now Gujarati, they know how to make veggy food.

I drive in this late summer day, to meet my first Indian cook, Mishti
from Gujarat.

Mishti lives in one of those apartment complexes, newly built, near
the area of Virginia known as Herndon. After meandering around the
parking lots, which all feed into each other and make no logical sense, I
finally find their ground floor garden apartment. I don't know Mishti: I
don't know if she is old, young, how educated; at this point, I don't even
know where she is from—it is a blank slate.

So I find her door, another portal of mystery. A tiny dried wreath of
flowers rests on its knocker.

And there she is, my newest guide to this soft world. Perhaps this
is the bittersweet feeling a man feels when he pays for a prostitute, that
this is something ideally you would have in your life naturally, and you
are paying for such a private rite, and there is probably such a sense of

vulnerability that you would need another human being, and yet a bit of pride that you did, after all, strike out and seek it.

And, yes, it is a need for a form of mothering.

My newly adopted mother, in this moment, is tiny and young, in her late twenties. Someone in the know told me Guju-babes are known for being sexy, that they tend to stay in shape. And such authority she possesses so young. She is elfin, gracious, and I leave my shoes by the door, which I always do in the Indian houses, and now I've come to think of it not just for cleanliness, but also as some meaningful ritual: as in, *who* you walk as in this world shall be left behind.

I have brought my son, not wanting to leave him at home. She gives him water and special sweets she brought from India, a golden hair-like candy that is delicate and saffrony, and crunchy hot biscuits. The apartment is simple, sparse, dotted with a few candles, and small icons of individuality, an altar to Ganesh in one corner, with a tiny brass frame of a family, blurry—I am unable to see more than the dim figures of a man, woman, a few kids of varying ages, amidst the dust of incense lying snaked on the table. The kitchen is merely a corner of the room, harshly lit by fluorescent. In the American need for convenience, have we achieved more time? No, not likely. Are we enjoying our meals? No, I don't think so. We are stripping ourselves of a basic sensuality that our bodies crave, touching our food, loving it before we sacrifice it. And we are longing to change this: food is hot right now. Classes are filling up, the TV networks are packed with shows teaching us how to go back to the basics.

A brief aside about Ganesh: how I am growing to adore him. Something about the Indian deity touches me, and I collect his figurines in my house. I love the fables about this elephant-faced, potbellied God. Most Indian homes will have a small Ganesh sculpture somewhere. He is heavily revered. He is supposed to be the first deity one worships in Hindu ceremonies called *pujas* (offerings), especially at the beginning of any venture, especially any creative venture, so perhaps that is why I have a fondness for him. He is considered the problem solver, and I've heard you can offer him a cracked coconut in particularly trying times. But it is a certain joviality and warmth that he seems to exude that I really love.

I am here to learn the basics. We wash vegetables and she is shy, diligent in her kindness. And she tells me of her home. She adds twice the amount of sliced green chilies to every dish, and tops it all with a spoon of sugar, a Gujarati trademark, she says.

We start with a spectacular dish called Saam Savera, or "morning evening." I had asked Indian friends about it when she emailed it to me, but nobody had heard of such a poetic dish. Small balls of mashed potato, seasoned with coriander powder, cilantro, and chopped green chili enclosed in a pocket of spinach, rolled in corn flour, deep fried, sliced in half and presented in a rich tomato based gravy. The whole dish is surreally beautiful, the black line on the edges, the green, the white, and the red, and I believe it is meant to conjure the look of the moon in the morning. It tastes so delicious. In addition, we learn how to make our own homemade Indian cheese, paneer. Quite simply, it is milk heated and curdled with lemon and then squeezed until it forms a solid block. This simple cheese is the basis for many Indian dishes.

Her husband, hair freshly washed, smiles up at me in a flash, as he sits on the carpet on his computer. Is there anything more beautiful than the look of wet, black hair? I've always been charmed by it. A soft peacefulness floats in this apartment, a sweet hammocky feeling of calm. They have no artwork, no fancy TVs. They are basic people and decorate with small symbols of their shared life: a magnet from Jamaica, a framed caricature of them both from another beach vacation, and small odds and ends which create the quilt of their lives. I can't help but see them and soak them in. I'm a spy of sorts.

Later, while sampling these lovely treats we have prepared, I ask her personal questions, as I tend to butt in whenever possible.

We have been married a year, she says when I ask.

My wife looks so young, doesn't she, says her husband, with pride and amusement; I look like an old man next to her.

But they are the same age and look it. I suppose he is telling me, Inside I feel so old. But I don't know why he would feel this way. I see him as one of the many bright stars from India, shiny-eyed, working in the tech world in new Virginia, a man whose old culture is only a whisper.

He leaves through the sliding glass door into the parking lot. His BMW is parked outside, glimmering even under the shade of the trees. The license plate says MIRACL BOY. Oh, I ask, impertinently, why is he a miracle boy?

She laughs a laugh that comes like muffled bells, and a tinge of reticence bathes it, Oh, because he is a miracle boy, she said, and I laugh, too, and I leave it at that, there is something so softly said, which is, You are not there yet. I perceive this subtlety and let it go.

And then I get to thinking: How we all do this dance. This stepping forward and pulling back, the hurting and loving we do our whole lives. And how I've come into her house, I've essentially invaded, I'm learning her family recipes, I'm cooking them, I'm eating them, I'm writing about them even, and even worse, I will enter and know more and more until I will know as much as I can. They will stand raw and naked, eyes bright, smiling. And they are freely giving.

And it just kills me. And then, I suppose we will love. And then, I can stay or just go away. And we deal with this all the time, don't we, this approaching, retreating, and think not much of it. But it seems to me so essential to us and who we are. I realize that I, too, must give, not just the twenty dollars that I give her at the end. This can't be a prostitution of culture, of food. It is given with her eyes looking into mine. I have to give myself as well.

I think about this during the week: I have to give.

I LAUGH WITH her during those two hours, and write all the details. And make plans for the next week. Her cooking is delightful and again, so different from my first teacher, Stella. Crested with her own style and tastes. She adds, as I've told you, a bit of sugar to everything, twice as many chilies it seems, and always a jarring dose of lemon juice. At first, I'm not used to these flavors in Indian cooking but as time goes by, I find I add them myself as well.

As the weeks go by, I have leaned a chockload of treats from her—a deliciously savory version of Mattar Paneer, the famous peas and cheese curry of Northern India—but without cream, simply bathed in an extremely spice-laden rich tomato-based gravy. A sumptuous stuffed okra dish with coconut. Malai Koftas, rich potato dumplings in a creamy soaked gravy. And one day, she produces Indian jewelry for me to see, and I buy a wedding set of extravagant turquoise jewelry. But it is a special day when we feast on a delicious assortment of chapathis that I have learned not so expertly to roll. She had pulled out the important skinny Indian rolling pin to create the ever-popular Aloo Paratha, a flat-bread filled with a savory potato stuffing, a staple item in any Northern Indian home, and a spicy paratha stuffed with shredded carrots, and for variety, a green chili paneer variety. We are tearing off large chunks and dipping them in curd and mint chutney. My lips are burning and I am having a serotonin high induced by all the green chilies.

Her husband, as usual freshly showered, comes padding on, usually to check the laptop on the sofa and then go wash his car.

There is a festival this weekend, if perhaps you would like to go, he says.

Yes, says Mishti, an Indian one.

Oh?

It is at our Krishna temple. You should come. There will be lots of foods and things.

I would like to understand more, so I ask her about this worship of Krishna, which is perceived as a cult in this country, merging with Hare Krishna. But I learn that they are followers of Vaishnavism, a devotion to Vishnu (God) as personified by Krishna. Who is Krishna? The eighth avatar, or incarnation of Vishnu, who is the all Supreme Being. Some say he is a Christ figure. As a young boy Krishna is the foster child of cowherds and shows his divine nature by conquering demons. As a youth he is the lover of the *gopis* (milkmaids), playing his flute and dancing with them by moonlight. The play of Krishna and the *gopis* is regarded in Hinduism as an image of the soul's relationship with God. The love of Krishna and Radha, his favorite *gopi*, is celebrated in a great genre of Sanskrit and Bengali love poetry. You will recognize him, if you ever look at devotional Hindu art, as the beautiful man with blue skin (Krishna means "black" in Sanskrit), with golden clothes and peacock plumes in his hat. And there is his most famous moment: with his friend, the great warrior Arjuna, about to go to battle. Arjuna turned to him and asked, Why should I fight? Where am I going after life? Whereupon, Krishna turned and thus spoke the famous scriptures: the Bhagavad Gita.

That night, I read about Krishna and Vaishnavism. I read the great principles, of which the first three are:

1. An absolute reality exists.

2. True success in life comes only by understanding reality and our place within it.

3. Science gives a limited picture of reality; abundant evidence
   suggests that part of reality exists beyond the reach of our senses
   and scientific instruments.

AND SO, I know learning to cook is a humble way to approach the whole idea of reality. There are transformational, alchemical natures to the act that imply spiritual initiations. A potato, given care, becomes much more than a potato. It becomes something sublime. It feeds us as we grow. Cooking, eating are the threads of our communal and family life.

The next week, Mishti and I are making potato and tomato curry. The smell of curry patta (fresh curry leaves) fills the air, an indescribable scent and flavor. This ingredient confuses Western cooks. Is that where curry powder comes from? No, curry powder is an English invention, and probably comes form the Tamil word for stew, *kari*. Curry leaves are from a small plant, the Sweet Neem, and have a smoky flavor and scent, almost mushroomy. And, of course, they are quite medicinal in Ayurveda, which is the traditional, native medicine of India that utilizes natural plants and herbs. Good for digestion and diabetes. The scent however has no words for description, but has a lovely warmth.

The usual car washing is happening in the parking lot. As we sit down to wait for the stew to cook, Mishti pulls out a large book.

What is this?

Our wedding pictures, she says.

I have not dared to ask if it is a love marriage or arranged, but whatever it is, it is working. One can feel the love between these two.

I have noticed their pictures do not festoon the wall like most couples.

Oh, she says in her perky voice, I keep meaning to put them up.

A yellow vinyl album is produced, with an airbrushed flower on the cover.

It is simple, and plain. Not like the large white silk and pearlized albums Americans would have. It is simple, until you open it up!

And then, she and her husband become the loveliest prince and princess one could ever imagine. I am quite honestly in awe, in the way one would be looking at the pictures of royalty from a fairy tale. She is covered in jewels, colors, and henna spirals in patterns on her hands. He is in a stoned turban, proud. Both are beautiful and golden. And then there is page after page of celebrations using old methods—the rubbing of turmeric, the women bringing terracotta pots of water to the party, the festive kaleidoscope of colors, platters of endless dishes and sweets. I find myself not quite jealous, too strong of a word. Colorless, lacking in spirit. As if I am Cinderella looking at the stepsisters' finery. I have been divorced for five years now. I have lost in some sense, my grounding as a woman. And did I ever have it? I am a victim and a beneficiary of my culture. I stand in such freedom, to go where I like, to be whom I like, to see anyone I wish. And yet, I feel uncared for, unloved. I feel I am not part of an endless web of relations, like these ones I see in jewels before me. I did not have a family decide my spouse, and perhaps, it would have been better. We are more free and yet, we are just lost in space, it seems.

I'm reaching out to be in the presence of connectedness as well, through the vehicle of food.

I see her family; her mother looks like a beautiful mature version of herself. And I see the groom, not in family shots. I see him standing ceremoniously in front of a framed picture. It is, it seems, the same picture I see in their altar with Ganesh and the incense. And where is his family? I ask, with innocence.

She smiles warmly and her eyes glisten.

Oh, she pauses. But she doesn't hesitate or leave me out. She tells me with all her heart.

They are passed away. They died in the earthquake of 2001.

Oh my God. I am so sorry. All of them?

Yes, all of them. The entire family. Except for Duli.

I look at her and back to the picture next to the frame.

Yes, he was there in the rubble. For five days.

There is a silence, not awkward, just appropriate.

The dal we are making has signaled it is ready for the next step with three insistent whistles from the pressure cooker. Life always intervenes.

I just say, I am so sorry and try to comprehend such a thing, but I can't.

And she told me with such openness, as if their story was now allowed to pass to me, as I had become a person to them. I felt honored.

As we added the tadka, which is the last finishing touch of spices to the dal, Mishti's husband Duli drives up to the parking space in front of the sliding glass door, his BMW newly washed and gleaming, the license plate clean and white: MIRACL BOY.

THE NEXT WEEKS pass by quickly as we sizzle and fry such delicacies. Mishti's spiciness has now suited my palate, and I welcome it. We move onto such wondrous dishes as Khadi, a very popular quick and easy yogurt sauce enjoyed in many Indian homes, flavored with a typical spice mixture, served with breads or rice. I realize this sauce is no doubt the origin of the "curry," doctored and hideously malshaped, we knew back in the '70s, brought over by English colonists. It is the creamed casserole party dish, with copious amounts of dusty lemon-colored curry powder and the little side dishes of raisins and peanuts. My grandmother made it, bathed in cream. And I learn chole, the chickpea curry, savory and spicy, a must for the everyday vegetarian, served with raised yeast bhature breads. I am taught to roll these with the lightest pressure, like the breath of a baby, very fast but very soft.

And then, one day I walk in to see a pile of odd boxes, from liquor stores.

Oh, are you moving, Mishti?

Yes, she says gleefully. We are going to Connecticut for relocation.

And then, by the end of the month, they are gone.

THE GANESH STATUE is always accompanied by a tiny mouse. Upon further investigation, I learn that the mouse symbolizes a minute vehicle for a cryptic subject. Because these small animals live in darkness, under the ground, it reminds us to always keep looking around, sniffing out knowledge, to illuminate ourselves with the inner light of wisdom.

I keep thinking about Duli. I really wanted to ask him something. One day, after they had found out I was a writer, Mishti called him from washing his BMW. She pattered on in Gujarati and he came running in. This was early on.

So you are a writer! he said.

Yes.

I love, you know, to go to Borders. Sit around reading. I'd like to write something one day. I have actually, he said, a good story in mind.

Now keep in mind everyone says this to writers, all the time, constantly.

Really? Well, why don't you write it?

Ohh, he laughed. No. I cannot.

We left it at that.

But I wanted to ask Duli later, after the wedding album moment, Tell me everything. How did you do it? How did you survive for five days? Did you have water? Did you hear your family? How did you sleep?

There are so many questions. I want to hug him, and say, God, man!

Only I can't. I just smile and say, Hi, as I stir okra curry.

He seems a different person now. In my eyes, he now possesses the distinction of tasting death, which I haven't. I truly believe if you have had this happen, you are different from others. Was I ever lying under the rubble of a building for five days? A writer is a very curious being. A human being has to, however, respect peace and be kind. So I often balance them, failing a lot of times, but in this case, I just don't feel I am quite there yet to ask and receive such knowledge. Now when I drive by their complex, missing those sessions cooking Gujarati food, I wonder on that. Mysteries are mysteries, I tell myself. Being mystery is enough, isn't it?

MISHTI LEAVES FOR Connecticut. They start a new life, with a few boxes. I miss them.

MISHTI'S MATTAR PANEER

This is the ever-popular dish of pea curry with cheese that you can find in most Indian buffets, but this version is spicy and doesn't contain the usual buckets of cream. In fact, it contains none at all, so it is a quite healthy and protein-rich main course.

- 2 cups of peas, either fresh or frozen (I find the organic variety infinitely better, but then organic anything usually is)
- 3 onions, preferably Vidalia
- 4 dried red chilies
- ¼ cup oil
- 2 tablespoons homemade ghee
- 6–7 cloves
- 2–3 bay leaves
- 1½ teaspoons red chili powder
- ½ teaspoon garam masala
- 3 tablespoons cumin powder
- 1 tablespoon coriander seeds, lightly toasted in a tawa or flat pan
- 4 garlic cloves
- 1 piece of ginger
- 1½ teaspoons salt
- 1½ cups fresh tomato puree
- About 3½ cups water
- 1 tablespoon fresh lemon juice
- 1 teaspoon sugar
- 2 teaspoons Kitchen King Masala (Optional. This is a store-bought masala that Mishti insisted adds a specific Punjabi taste. It does taste delicious. I've tried to find the recipe to make my own to no avail.)

Grind garlic, onions, and ginger together with the coriander seeds in a food processor until smooth, the consistency of applesauce. Place a large saucepan on medium-high heat, and after about 5 minutes, add oil and ghee. Place the cloves, bay leaves, and red chilies in the oil and let them darken to a mahogany shade. These are referred to as the "whole" garam masala, as opposed to ground garam masala. At this point, add the garlic-onion-ginger paste. Stir for about 15 minutes. You really want it to dry out and become a nice golden caramel color and for the oil to come out around the edges. This process will really add a lot of flavor. It will take about 15 minutes and don't rush it! Add red chili powder, ground garam masala, cumin powder, tomato puree, and water. Add salt, cover and let simmer rapidly for about 10 minutes. This will mature the gravy. Add 2 green chilies, about ½ cup more water and Kitchen King Masala. Boil for 10 more minutes. Add peas and paneer, sugar and lemon juice. Let meld together on medium-low heat for 15 minutes. The sauce should have a thick consistency, like that of a stew. Add a tad more water if it thickens too much.

This is perfectly fine to be made a day ahead, although the Ayurvedic tradition frowns upon this as the food loses vitality. It is classically served with a bread, such as chapathi, in the North, although rice is fine as well. Basically, Mishti taught me northern food with a Guju twist.

MISHTI'S SAAM SAVERA

"Morning Evening" is a Mughlai dish of spinach koftas and spiced gravy, so named because these koftas or dumplings, when sliced, resemble the moon in early twilight.

- 1 bunch fresh spinach, well-washed, tough stems removed, and blanched in 3 cups of salted, boiling water, squeezed dry and roughly chopped
- 1 batch homemade paneer (a dry goat's cheese could be substituted)
- 1 teaspoon red chili powder
- 2 tablespoons corn flour
- ½ teaspoon salt
- 1 green serrano chili
- 1 teaspoon garam masala
- 2 tomatoes, roughly chopped
- 1 red onion, roughly chopped
- 2-inch piece of ginger, roughly chopped
- 2 garlic cloves, roughly chopped
- 2 teaspoons coriander power
- 1 teaspoon cumin powder
- 1 tablespoon honey
- 1 tablespoon sour cream
- ½ cup water
- 2 tablespoons dried methi (fenugreek)

Season spinach with salt, ½ teaspoon of red chili powder, and 1 tablespoon corn flour. Mix well. Add more corn flour if it is too soft. Crumble paneer and shape into small balls the size of walnuts. Take a golf ball size of spinach, flatten in your palm and place a paneer ball on the spinach. Shape the spinach around the ball and squeeze tight to enclose. Place on a plate in the refrigerator.

Grind the tomatoes, ginger, onion, and garlic together in a food processor or blender to make a salsa texture. Heat oil in a large pan and add mixture. Cook over medium-high heat until oil shows around edges, about 15 minutes. Add coriander powder and garam masala. Stir well. Add sour cream, honey, and methi. Stir well. Add water and let simmer.

Meanwhile, heat oil to 350°F. Roll spinach balls in corn flour and carefully dip them in heated oil for 5 minutes. Remove to paper towels. They should be dark on outside. To serve, slice spinach balls in half carefully with very sharp knife. Heat sauce and place koftas on the sauce. Serve with chapathi, rotis, or puris.

MISHTI'S KADHI WITH DUMPLINGS

Besan or chickpea flour fritters stewed in a yogurt sauce. Quite delicious and nutritious.

FOR PAKORAS (DUMPLINGS):
- ¾ cup besan (chickpea flour)
- ½ cup water
- ½ teaspoon red chili powder
- ½ teaspoon baking powder
- ½ cup red onion, chopped
- ½ cup spinach, chopped
- ½ teaspoon salt

FOR SAUCE:
- 1 cup plain yogurt
- ⅔ cup besan (chickpea flour)
- ¼ teaspoon turmeric powder
- 6 cups water
- 2 tablespoons ghee or oil
- 1 teaspoon cumin seeds
- 1 teaspoon mustard seeds
- 1 red chili
- 3 bay leaves
- ½ teaspoon fenugreek
- A pinch of asafetida (hing)

FOR THE PAKORAS (DUMPLINGS):
Mix the besan and water together until it is very smooth and resembles a thick icing for a cake. Add more water if it is too dry. Beat this for 3 minutes, until it becomes fluffy. Add remaining ingredients. Place small teaspoon balls in hot oil (375°F). To test, you can also just drop a small piece of dough in the oil, and if

it pops up immediately it is ready. You can use a spoon. Mishti used her hand. After a minute, flip them and make sure they brown on both sides.

Remove to paper towel, and cool for 5 minutes. Place in a bowl of room temperature water and soak for 10 minutes. After that, remove by handfuls and squeeze out water gently. Place into Kadhi Sauce and cook on medium-low for 10 minutes to meld flavors. Serve with white basmati rice.

FOR THE SAUCE:
Beat besan and yogurt until very smooth—take time with this as it is very important the mixture is smooth. Slowly add 3 cups of water; it should be like a light pancake batter. Heat oil in pan and add cumin, mustard seeds, fenugreek, red chili, and bay leaves to sizzle. Add asafetida, turmeric, and salt. Add yogurt mixture to pan and stir well. Let this come to a boil and add 3 more cups of water. When it boils, turn down to medium-low and cook for 1 hour. Add pakoras to sauce to heat through, and serve with white basmati rice.

MISHTI'S POTATO AND TOMATO CURRY

A traditional Gujarati dish, present at all functions and dinners.

* 6 medium white potatoes, peeled, boiled, and crushed by hands into small pieces
* 1 large red onion, finely chopped
* 2 cloves garlic, chopped
* 1-inch piece of ginger, finely chopped
* ½ teaspoon mustard seeds
* 2 dried red chilies
* 10–12 curry leaves
* 2 green chilies, cut into rounds
* ½ teaspoon red chili powder
* 2 teaspoons coriander powder
* 1 teaspoon cumin powder
* ¼ teaspoon turmeric powder
* ½ teaspoon salt, or according to taste
* 3 medium tomatoes, finely chopped
* 2 tablespoons oil
* 1 tablespoon sugar
* 2 tablespoons lemon juice
* Chopped coriander leaves for garnish

Heat oil in a pan, add the mustard seeds, and let them sizzle. Now add the red chilies and curry leaves, and stir-fry for a few seconds. This is called "bhuna," the roasting of spices (see page 210). Add onions, ginger, and garlic and cook until the onions turn light brown, about 10 minutes. Add the tomatoes and stir-fry until the oil separates and appears on the sides. Add the green chilies, other spices, and salt. Add the potatoes and simmer on low heat for 5 minutes.

Add 1 cup of water to the mix. Let this simmer on low heat until it appears thickened, like a stew. Add sugar, lemon, and cilantro.

Serve hot with white rice or breads.

Bollywood and Bitter Melon

Heroes and heroines in the war of love

I AM MOURNING THE loss of Mishti and her spicy Gujarati influenced northern food. I find myself making it and adding the lemon and sugar as she would. Fall has come and pumpkins are everywhere. I am having a birthday in a few weeks. I will be forty-six.

I feel lonely and ungrounded, taking care of my kids, yet collapsing each evening in exhaustion. I seem to be juggling too many things and losing balance.

But I received more responses to the ad, so I contact one of them, a woman who calls herself Meena. She leads me to Vienna, a posh neighborhood in Northern Virginia, west of DC. In general this area had been developed in the '70s and not much has been renovated since. A staleness of design hovers over the strip malls and shops as you drive through. Archaic hues of brown and tan, dated rooftops, and bad shrubbery quietly offend. I find my way, via MapQuest as always, to a Starsky & Hutch–like condo building, with patios and sliding glass doors that inevitably stick. I come to the ground floor of one such apartment.

Meena is small and pleasantly fleshy, with a gleaming round face and the kind of mouth that stretches from the outer corner of each cheek impossibly. She is apologetic for her home, there seem to be piles of books and clutter everywhere and in the midst of this, a sad floral couch, a few boxes of Christmas ornaments, and in the middle of the room a small fake tree. It is a small place and they've only been there a year, she says.

I don't know anyone here, she says, for this reason I thought this would be a good idea.

It is then I realize a familiar theme: a lot of these ladies are responding because of loneliness. They don't know any Americans here. They want to connect. The cooking part seems to reassure them and their husbands that it will be safe.

And strangely, for me it is the same. I also want to connect.

Her husband emerges, a bright, funny guy who hangs around and then retreats to a laptop. It is a useful device, the men can oversee the event lightly from the computer, while actually responding to a few emails.

Meena's kitchen is tiny and squeezed into a wall. There is a table wedged in between a desk and a small TV, and again, there are piles of papers and DVDs, mainly Bollywood flicks.

I like to watch the Bollywood movies when I cook, she explains.

Oh, she is crazy about them, says her husband from the couch, she watches all day long. I try and tell her to get out, do something, but—

I love them, she says quietly.

And when I ask her favorites, she brightens like a flame and lists all the stars, but I don't know them. I see her wedding pictures as magnets on the refrigerator and she is all in red, a goddess. I ask about the wedding.

By now, he has come over, bubbling with details.

Oh, it was a grand affair. It went for seven days. We had four hundred people. Her family is very fine people.

She is glowing.

By now, she is sizzling cloves, whole red chili, cardamom, and bay leaves—whole garam masala—to flavor the oil. You will notice in recipes that garam masala, literally "warm spices," are used in various ways, either whole or ground, and sometimes both. She lets them darken considerably. The air fills with the sharp burn of chili and we all cough in that half-choked way one does with chili oil. Meena is making chole, the delicious chickpea stew that is a mainstay for Indian vegetarians, especially those in the North, in Punjab, though Meena and her husband are from Pondicherry, in the South, thus the signs around the house that they are Christians. Meena teaches me northern delicacies because her mother is northern. They tell me everyone likes chole. Traditionally, it should have a dark tone, so some people add tea, she says. I knew that, having read it somewhere. Tea adds the preferred dark color quickly. But, says Meena, I prefer just to let the onions cook down properly and they will add the color. At this point, after she has added the pureed onion, ginger, and garlic, the house fills with such a colorful streamer of scents. Meena has added spices, the ground coriander, turmeric, cumin, and chili powder, followed by fresh tomato puree. Now it must all cook until the oil escapes from the pulp of the tomato. He has put on some contemporary Indian music, with the characteristic high pitch of the female voice.

Would you like some chai, she asks.

Of course I agree and she slices chunks of ginger into a pan and here I learn the secret of Meena's Chai. I relish a steaming cup of the stuff.

The husband wants to stay away and yet he can't. My sense is that he also is lonely here and bored. An interesting stranger has entered the scene. They are truly friendly people and love to tell me all about their culture. Frankly, I think he is a bit into me as well, a slight attraction to this woman who has come into their lives, though he is polite and respectful. I feel slightly uncomfortable. My sense is that this marriage is not too happy. And, roundabout, we somehow come to talk of marriage.

Their marriage was arranged.

He tries to explain, thinking I will find it archaic and useless as a methodology. I don't. It depends on your expectations. Who am I to criticize? I am divorced. And I am not of their culture. The idea, however, of my parents rooting out a reasonable choice for me amongst my peers is humorous. My parents are liberal, artistic ex-bohemians, who forage for mushrooms in their spare time, played Jimi Hendrix while I grew up, and attended anti-war rallies. Who would they have picked?

No, I was on my own for that one, a choice that may be the most important choice of your life. I, like all my friends, was given no advice, no tips. We had no over-meddling mother who led us as debutantes to the best men of our league, fresh from college, as happened in my grandmother's age. In her time, a young girl of eighteen bought a new wardrobe and gave a party to announce, I am ready to marry, everyone! And men would line up as suitors. They would visit with flowers. Take you to dances. Perhaps steal a kiss. And then, they would visit your father for your hand.

No, I was adrift in the '70s, post-sexual-revolution America. You had boyfriends. There was no talk of marriage. You talked of your personal goals or, at best, what to do for the weekend. You fought. You made love. Then you broke up. And you went to the next one.

And then I was twenty-eight, twenty-nine. It was not that I decided to marry. It was more a general change came in the air, like when fall descends. One doesn't decide to end summer, it just comes. You put on a coat. The snow comes. I grew weary of relationships or maybe my internal biological clock was nudging me, I don't know. I met a man who seemed good for me, nice, funny. We shared the same interests. We were different religions and temperaments, yet I ignored this. It seemed good at the time. It wasn't so much a choice as the subtle drifting of a raft on the water. I floated along, but happily. A ring appeared, I wore it, then I planned a large party, and in one instant I became a wife. Was love involved? Yes, it was. But did it last? Sadly no. This is the argument of the arranged marriage set, that these initial emotions are probably lust or infatuation and rarely last. Love, it is said, lasts forever.

She shows me with pride a small picture of her in the traditional red sari, beaming.

It was all very nice, she says.

Her husband goes to halfheartedly place a few ornaments here and there on the tree, as he gleefully recounts their big day:

In the mornings, her butler was just frying puri after puri, bringing them out in trays for us to devour. Oh, I could have eaten them all day.

Whoever has a butler, I think to myself.

It seems to me that life has deflated a bit for them since the big event.

By now Meena has added the chickpeas, a bit of water, some dried mango powder for acidity to the chole, and the whole thing is bubbling. She is showing me how to roll small rounds of puris like her butler in Pondicherry did. Magically, they puff up into steamed balls. When the chole is ready, we scoop it up with torn pieces of puri.

The next time I go we watch *Dilwale Dulhania Le Jayenge*, a Bollywood classic, she says, and we make rajma (kidney bean curry) with cumin rice. I notice she tears up at one point, but I politely ignore it. I too love the movie for all of its over the top romanticism. By the end of the movie, our steaming hot rajma is ready and we eat it with rice. *The Lover Will Take the Bride* is its name. All Bollywood movies seem to be thwarted love stories, couples destined for each other but promised to others. I wondered if Meena felt this inside her. I knew I would never know.

From my writing students, I have learned this is a very common theme, judging from the amount of stories from men and women that I see: *the one that got away.* Usually, the end of the romance is due to school ending or some kind of life transition, not so much from lack of feeling. And the person pines for them for the rest of his or her life. Of course, in the end of this movie, everyone is happy. In real life, well, not so much. Somehow I couldn't help but wonder: Did Meena have a romantic chip inside her? Do we all?

I OFTEN THINK of Meena, how she watches the Bollywood films. The movies always culminate with a resplendent wedding on the grandest Indian scale, such as the one Meena had before she moved here. Despite the veneer of artificial happiness that she and her husband tried to project, I detected an underlying sadness in her. Something about how she watched the movies, as if she craved fantasy and romance.

By the way, in Bollywood parlance, *heroes* and *heroines* are movie stars, male and female respectively. I didn't know this before.

She asked me, Who is your favorite hero?

Hero? I said. I don't know. Gandhi?

Extreme laughter.

Maybe Nelson Mandela. Oh, Muhammad Yunus—

More cackling from Meena.

What, she doesn't know about Muhammad Yunus, the economist from Pakistan who revolutionized micro banking?

What the—?

She explained.

The last day I am with her she promises to teach me Bitter Melon next time.

No bitter melon, her husband says, Americans won't like this.

Yes, I will, I say.

We will see about that.

But then an email comes and they want twice the money for teaching. I have to decline.

I feel bad for Meena.

And for me. I guess we'll never know if I liked Bitter Melon.

MEENA AND HER husband had no altars to Ganesh in their small apartment. They had a cross on one wall, a Christmas tree, and a small framed picture of feminine folded hands, with a cursive script prayer underneath, gracing the house.

As I walked in from a day with them, I held the plastic containers of her Malai Koftas and puris, so well-made and tasty, as well as a few scrawled pages of the recipes. She had given me so much, her story and her food, and tales of her happiness (and unhappiness). My Ganesh statue sits in an enclave in my home, surrounded by flowers, and I light a stick of Tibetan healing incense. I tried to be thankful for the gifts of that day. Ganesh has many physical characteristics, one most notably is his distinct potbelly, which it is said contains infinite universes and signifies much. First and foremost, nature and equanimity, and his ability to swallow the sorrows of the Universe and protect the world. I have suffered from Ganesh syndrome most of my life—i.e., even when I am slim, I always have a small pooch on my tummy. I've basically always hated it, and dream, now that I've had two kids and the small pooch is more of a pillow, of having a tummy tuck one of these days. But sometimes, looking at Ganesh, I feel a sense of pride on some level, that this part of me has reproduced life and also represents my taste for life. And I wonder, which is better, alone and adrift like myself, or companioned yet definitely aching, like Meena and her husband. Perhaps Ganesh will open the doors to this mystery as well.

But Meena moves on, and so do I.

Still alone, but starting to cook really well.

Especially good chai.

MEENA'S CHAI

* 1 cup milk
* ½ cup water
* 1 black tea bag
* 3 slices of ginger
* 6 cloves
* 1 piece of cinnamon stick
* A pinch of crushed cardamom seeds
* 3 teaspoons brown sugar.

Combine all ingredients in a saucepan and cook the chai until it boils rapidly for 5 minutes. Turn down for 5 minutes, and then strain. Delicious.

MEENA'S MALAI KOFTAS

These are the vegetarian alternative to meatballs made of potatoes, cheese, and vegetables in a rich cashew gravy. Delicious with puris, nan, or cumin rice. Vegans can eliminate cream in the sauce and substitute soft tofu for the paneer.

FOR KOFTAS:
- 1½ cups paneer, grated (or use 1 mashed soft tofu block)
- 3 small russet potatoes, boiled, peeled, and mashed
- 1 cup green peas
- 1 small carrot, boiled and grated
- ½ cup corn, cooked
- 1 teaspoon garam masala
- 1 teaspoon coriander powder
- 1 teaspoon cumin powder
- ½ teaspoon red chili powder
- 1 tablespoon fresh lemon juice
- 2 teaspoons Kitchen King Masala
- 3–4 tablespoons besan (chickpea flour)
- 2 tablespoons cashews, roughly chopped
- 3 tablespoons golden raisins, roughly chopped
- 1½ teaspoon salt
- 2 tablespoons cilantro, chopped
- 1 green chili (serrano or jalapeño), chopped
- ¾ cup toasted plain bread crumbs
- Oil for deep-frying, plus 2 tablespoons

FOR GRAVY:
- Whole garam masala: 1-inch cinnamon stick, 2 whole green cardamom pods, 2 whole cloves, 1 bay leaf
- 2 medium onions, finely chopped
- 4 tomatoes, pureed

* 1-inch piece of ginger, chopped
* 2 garlic cloves, chopped

FOR SPICE PASTE:
* ½ cup cashews, chopped
* 1 teaspoon garam masala
* 2 teaspoons Kitchen King Masala
* 2 teaspoons cumin powder
* 1 tablespoon coriander powder
* ½ teaspoon red chili powder
* 1 teaspoon turmeric powder
* 1 cup whipping cream (you can use ½ cup yogurt instead—different flavor but very good, or you can skip this part if you are vegan)
* 1 tablespoon tandoori masala or paneer masala
* 1 tablespoon oil or ghee
* 2 tablespoons fresh cilantro leaves, finely chopped
* 1 tablespoon honey
* 1 teaspoon salt or to taste

FOR THE KOFTAS:

Mix all kofta ingredients—except for nuts and raisins—in a bowl using your hands or use a potato masher. Make sure the vegetables are blended. Do not add water. Mash very well. The consistency should be that of chunky mashed potatoes. Using the 2 tablespoons of oil, moisten hands lightly with a few drops to prevent sticking. Make small golf ball sized balls and flatten in your palm. Add ½ teaspoon of raisins and nuts in the middle and close up into a firm ball. Make sure it is tight and firm. Heat oil to medium-high (360°F). Roll balls in bread crumbs and fry in batches until golden brown. If they are falling apart, stop, and add more besan to the mix.

Put aside on a paper towel for draining.

These can be served as appetizers with coriander-mint chutney and tamarind-date chutney.

FOR THE GRAVY:
Heat oil in pan and add whole garam masala. Let sizzle and turn light brown. Add onions, garlic, ginger, and tomatoes to food processor and blend until consistency of applesauce. Pour into pan, being careful not to let splatter. Add salt. Stir and cook for 15 minutes, or until oil appears around edges of sauce, stirring frequently.

In blender mix cashews, Kitchen King Masala, cumin, coriander powder, ground garam masala, chili powder, and turmeric powder into smooth paste with 3 tablespoons water to create a spice paste. Add to the pan with the onion-tomato mix. Add 1½ cups water to blender to remove traces of cashew mix and add to pot. Let cook for 5 minutes to meld flavors. Add cream, honey, and paneer masala, and stir well. Cook for 10 minutes. Right before serving, sprinkle in cilantro. Place koftas in sauce just to heat, for a few minutes, otherwise they will fall apart. Serve with chapathis or Mattar Pulao (peas and rice). This is very festive.

MEENA'S RAJMA

* 1 cup rajma (dark red kidney beans), soaked overnight or at least 8 hours (or 1 large can, 13 ounces)
* 1 red onion, chopped
* 1-inch piece of ginger, chopped
* 4 tomatoes, chopped
* 1 teaspoon cumin seeds
* 1 small cinnamon stick
* 1 teaspoon turmeric powder
* 1 teaspoon cumin powder
* 1 teaspoon garam masala powder
* 1 tablespoon ghee
* 2 tablespoons coriander leaves, chopped
* 2 tablespoons vegetable or sunflower oil
* 1 teaspoon salt or to taste

Cook the soaked rajma in about 3 cups of water in a pot or a pressure cooker until four whistles. Or about 25 minutes. In a blender or food processor puree onions, garlic, tomatoes, and ginger until salsa consistency. Heat oil in a saucepan, add cumin seeds and cinnamon stick, and allow to sizzle and pop. Add ginger, onion, and garlic mixture. Sauté until onions are soft and golden brown, about 15 minutes.

Add turmeric powder, cumin powder, garam masala powder and sauté for a few minutes. Add the cooked rajma, salt, 1 cup water, and ghee, simmer for 30 minutes. Garnish with coriander leaves and chopped tomato and serve hot with jeera (cumin) rice.

MISHTI'S JEERA RICE

This is an unusual lemony version that I learned from Mishti, actually, but it goes well with Meena's Rajma.

- ¼ cup canola oil
- 2 onions, sliced in half and then in long slivers
- 2 tablespoons cumin seeds
- 2 green chilies
- 1 teaspoon ginger, grated
- 1 teaspoon garlic, grated
- 2 tablespoons lemon juice
- 1 teaspoon sugar
- 2 cups basmati rice
- 5 cups water
- Salt to taste
- 2 tablespoons cilantro leaves, chopped

Heat oil in a pan and add cumin seeds. Let them sizzle. Add onions, grated ginger, garlic, and green chilies. Fry till onions turn slightly brown. Add rice and fry for 2 minutes. Add water and salt. Let boil for 5 minutes or until water starts to dry up and soak into rice. Cover with a cloth dishtowel (careful with edges, fold them over the lid) and a tight cover. Steam on low for 15 minutes. Uncover, fluff, and add 1 teaspoon ghee if desired, lemon juice, and sugar. This is a Gujarati touch—you can eliminate sugar and lemon juice. Garnish with coriander leaves.

Sour Tamarind and Sweet Talk

It is wrong to think that love comes from long companionship
and persevering courtship. Love is the offspring of spiritual
affinity and unless that affinity is created in a moment,
it will not be created for years or even generations.

—KAHLIL GIBRAN

ND THEN CAME Sarasvati.

Let me say that by this point I feel I have the basics of Indian food somewhat accomplished, and yet as I go along I realize I could study this for the rest of my days and barely scratch the surface.

But there are a few important steps which really make a difference: cooking down the initial sauce base until well-cooked before adding the spices, knowing the right time to add spices, and adding the final garnishing spices known as tadka, at the end. This series of spicing elements seems to layer the flavors appropriately according to the property of each flavor. In the same way, my role of spiritual seeker will continue by layering and exploring different flavors. There are so many cultural expressions of spirituality in the world, and in my opinion, all are worthy and educational. It is the twisting and misuse of man's ego that damages the beauty of most religious theory, but in essence all the great books talk similarly of the unknown mystery that we would refer to as God.

Both paths require respect—the path of cooking a respect for the ingredients and for whom you will serve. Can you cook well for someone you don't like? I don't think so.

Similarly, in terms of spirituality, can we expect to learn anything if we don't respect others ways and traditions?

And yet, while a Christian will openly talk of her faith if asked and in fact, proselytize, as some branches actually demand, a Hindi will guard her ways with a certain reticence, afraid that one might judge, or misuse. There is perhaps a feeling that people like myself may simply skim the surface of a thousands-of-years-old way of life. Not wanting to offend, I ask when there is an opening, or I read. When someone wants to teach me, he can. I won't even quote that old saw about when the "student is ready." Like a sushi chef in training who is only allowed to sweep the floors for the first year, I try and simply make dal. Over and over again, I make dal. To simply learn this one thing well, I cook it often. Simply. Understanding the spices and the smells. Following my nose and other senses.

Enjoying its simple purity.

Since I started learning with these ladies, I have acquired equipment—a masala dabba (well worth obtaining, see Tools, page 211), an Indian rolling pin, and a pressure cooker. Actually, I did not buy the pressure cooker. The pressure cooker was brought to me, wrapped in tissue, escorted through thousands of miles over land and sea.

So now I will tell you the long and arbitrary yet meaningful way I obtained an Indian pressure cooker:

The Hindu Goddess Sarasvati is the goddess of art: music, painting, sculpture, dance, and writing. She is especially the goddess of writing, because she gifted writing to mankind so that her songs could be written down and preserved. Sarasvati is the daughter of Lord Shiva and

Goddess Durga. She has four hands representing four aspects of human personality in learning: mind, intellect, alertness, and ego. She has sacred scriptures in one hand and a lotus—the symbol of true knowledge—in the second. She wears a white sari—a symbol of purity—and rides a white swan. Given all that, when a woman would have such a name, one would expect a goddess of tradition.

But, no. Sara, as she is called, is anything but. Thoroughly modern, a slim sprite with long dark hair and a pursed mouth. Sharp as a blade, thin. She meets me at the door, wary. I don't know why. Her hair piled on top, thin rimless glasses atop a proud nose.

She's in her late twenties, unmarried, an executive, a top consultant. Why she asked me to come I don't know, but I assume just for fun. She tells me she is only here occasionally, that her brother is staying with her, and she is on the road much. She is Punjabi, northern, regal, tall, and angular, as they tend to be.

I enter a house stark and empty, brand new, with gleamingly modern furniture in what feng shui would call metal energy—cool grays, silvers, blacks. This is not a frilly house, but a place of work and study—a place of—

From the kitchen, her brother enters.

Have you ever seen a wolf, truly in real life or any animal caught in the wild, perhaps walking? Not in a zoo, but caught in their natural habitat. Have you ever been in the presence of something naturally wild, unfettered?

I have an affinity for foxes. I saw one by the winding country road I was driving on once, and I stopped the car next to it. He didn't run away. He was incredibly close and I turned off the engine. There was this long intense moment of complete stillness as we recognized each other. He did not run. He stood and looked at me, really looked at me deeply with his pale golden eyes. Motionless. After some time I tried to bark as foxes do. I used to hear them from my house when I grew up, a sharp, flat, raspy jet of sound. He listened. After a good five minutes, I started the car and drove away.

He did not move.

There is a very different quality to meeting something of such wilderness, such attention. This man, this boy, walked in, and I felt very disarmed and paralyzed. Our eyes locked. They would not unlock. His bold eyes were undauntingly intense, with a deep black glare. And yet, they projected innocence of the highest degree. Purity, like that fox.

My friend Layla and I have been having a long-standing conversation—the one that rehashes, again and again, the difference between mind-thinking and heart-thinking. Rational thinking certainly has its place—we often need to weigh consequences and facts and make careful decisions, perhaps when buying a house or deciding on a school. But there is also the very relevant area of heart-thinking, where in a mere second one's own higher self recognizes and evaluates what is essential. For all the research I may do on comparing houses in a desired neighborhood, my experience always has been that when I find the right one, it feels peaceful instantly. I believe this form of judgment is really significant when dating—if it has to be analyzed through the head too much, a sort of inner weighing of pros and cons with a potential mate, I suspect the pairing has its issues. I have, like most people, experience in both areas, and have now, in my wise older years, come back to wanting my initial sense of immediacy and peace. If I am going on a date, I trust the brooding, uncomfortable sensation in the pit of my stomach, not as nerves but as incompatibility, and most times I am right.

But what does one do when that "good" feeling occurs—the natural, flowing, and clean sense of truth—and yet, physically, reasonably, logically, in the world we live in, this person represents an incompatible choice for your life? Does one follow the mind or the heart?

Let us examine food, since I always seem to come back to that: Does one need to spend a lifetime either choosing all junk food, which is horrible and unhealthy, or always sacrifice and eat a spare, deprived diet that seems healthy yet offers no joy? Or perhaps, might you follow your instincts—feeling your body's needs when it requires something (I crave spinach often, when low on iron) and yet also allowing what brings simple joyfulness in and of itself—a piece of chocolate, a delightful fresh tomato off the vine, a fine glass of wine—to obtain a balance of soul and mind. Essentially, I ask: If we are not set up when born for the perfect set of tools, to eat and eliminate, to procreate, to ambulate, are we not also born with the intrinsic guidance that leads us to health and happiness?

SARA BROUGHT ME in to the kitchen, offered me tea, and I felt shaken, a bit scared. I was moved by a very young man, and despite all my nature talk here, I do not think of myself as a "cougar," a predatory woman who seeks younger men. I have been only with men my own age or older. I find the concept foreign, uncomfortable. It seems to awaken a lot of stale ideas: that I would be the "mother," that I am afraid of aging, or that it would seem to other people that it was all about sex—I don't know, I try and review these ideas later, when it is too late. Because some things in life feel as inevitable as an avalanche that has started, a falling crescendo of events.

In one moment, I saw a very wild thing and in the same moment I also saw a very gentle person, with the calm brow of a monk. I felt an instant connection. Call it what you will, biology, immaturity, whatever your science can explain, to me it felt otherworldly. Immediate connection, not only physical but spiritual.

We talked briefly about me being an author. He was delighted by this. We exchanged pleasantries but they felt like tiny mosquitoes flying around a giant elephant. A burning vortex existed now between us. And this elephant would not be still. He brimmed with power, he stood poised to recklessly stampede the house and his wild brooding smell filled the room.

Yet, still the tiny buzzing of mosquitoes: So where do you go to school? You are an author! You like to cook Indian food?

He excused himself to go study. Study! He was a college student! Shame filled my face at even thinking in this way. I swallowed and grew up.

Then, I put down the spatula as Sara went to the bathroom. I can see the shadow of his body against the doorway from behind the curtain of my hair. I look up, our eyes meet.

Try and imagine a piercing elephant trumpet at this point, blasting in the plain soft walls of suburbia.

SARA WAS SYSTEMATIC and so kind, insisting on giving me two scarves from India that I tried to push away, but she said, Please! Please! And so I kept them.

She taught me about bottle gourd, too.

Koftas are the meatballs of the vegetarians, prevalent in every form and variety, and I still can't find any as soft and delectable as Sara's bottle gourd variety. What the heck is bottle gourd? you ask. Well, it is a very popular Indian vegetable, resembling a huge overgrown pale zucchini. In fact, you can substitute zucchini in this recipe if you wish. Because it holds a lot of water, it needs to be squeezed dry first, before cooking. Bottle gourd is one of these healthy Ayurvedic vegetables—full of iron, vitamins C and B; it also is a liver cleaner, cares for the urinary tract, soothes the stomach, and is good for the eyes.

She grated the large bottleneck and rolled quick little koftas, while he drifted around our periphery.

She taught me the Punjabi delights they had grown up on: Bottle gourd (ghia) kofta, kheer, Kadhai Pakora, Sooji Halvah. Kheer is rice pudding, and absolutely luscious. One can't attend a wedding or an auspicious event without a bowl of this somewhere, I am told, and I can see why: It is both comforting and nourishing, yet exhilarating, with cardamom and nuts, a touch of saffron if you wish. Diwali, the festival of lights, commemorates the victory of good over evil. It is also the day when Lakshmi, the consort of Vishnu and the goddess of prosperity, is worshipped. Lakshmi and Vishnu are said to live in the celestial Kheersagar (the ocean of milk). This is the origin of the dish kheer. The preparation of kheer is a must on Diwali.

Sara's version is full of nuts and fruits, though I have tried many with just cardamom or saffron or rosewater. Experiment and see which one suits you. Basmati rice is preferred because it is very delicate and breaks down, leaving a creamy texture without too much rice flavor.

He stared at me, saying nothing. Our glance didn't break. Long, strange minutes went by. What was happening?

Sara walked back in.

So, how is the kheer.

Very nice, I said. My voice was very small, a mere breath.

LATER THAT NIGHT, I went to check my email.

hi wats up?

Somehow he had obtained my email from his sister. In the younger generation texting style, came a request asking me to go to a wine bar. *i know i am really young n stuff but i jus want someone to talk to.* Appalling! A wine bar! He did not drink. He would say "u" for you and "whaevah" and such. I refused to meet him.

But we started talking, frequently. We would look down and realize we had spoken for hours, which had breezed by. We talked mostly about religion, God, higher abstract concepts while our connection also burned on a very simple physicality, even through the phone. I could literally feel the intensity. We seemed to agree on most things; he, like myself, questioned and pondered. We exchanged music, readings. I sent him some Wagner. He sent me MC Punjabi.

HE AND SARA had no Ganesh in the house, or cross, or Durga Altar. They were not Muslim; there were no framed calligraphic passages of the Q'uran in Arabic.

Sara and V, as I'll call him, were Radhasoami, something I had never heard of. A current website calls it a "science of the soul" and describes it as such:

> The philosophy teaches a personal path of spiritual development which includes a vegetarian diet, abstinence from intoxicants, a moral way of life and the practice of daily meditation. There are no rituals, ceremonies, hierarchies or mandatory contributions, nor are there compulsory gatherings. Members need not give up their cultural identity or religious preference to follow this path.

I AM INTERESTED. He says he will give me some books. I say that would be nice, but. I do not want to meet him. He insists. I say no.

I stop meeting with his sister. I have a new teacher and anyway, Sara is traveling most of the time. He calls me for two weeks, asking to meet. Most times however, we talk for hours. He explains the Radhasoami way, he tells me how he came here. How he missed a few points from the all important testing to get into IIT, the technology school of India, which was his dream and sent him into a deep desperation, whereas he lost significant weight, lying in his room for days on end. Finally, he moved to the U.S. without saying anything to his parents—essentially running away.

He found himself now in the cold suburbs of Virginia attending a community college, trying to make good grades so he can transfer to his dream—Wharton School of business—and make something of himself. And he found himself talking to a forty-something American woman, an aunty, as I would be called in India.

I've never had anyone in my life, he said.

I think to myself, you haven't *lived* your life.

IT IS MY birthday. I am with six good friends having sushi in Washington DC. We are singing karaoke and having fun, drinking sake, a cake arrives with candles, not forty-six of them, but three, which will do.

My phone is chiming with texts:

come w me 2nt. lez go to va beach. i nvr hv gone to the ocen. lez driv all nite.

I ignore. Blow out the candles, happy birthday to youooooo! Happy birthday to youooooo!

pls I want to spnd time w u.

My friend Layla thinks I am insane. She says it's immoral, and wrong. Partly I agree, partly I am simply too captivated. And anyway, she's been in love with a man fourteen years her junior for nine years, so come on. Another friend at the table, Helen, a Brit, is amused: Darling, bravo! she says. Most women my age are curious, intrigued. While we would love to be wooed by a sexy, younger man, what would happen? Or some need more security, like Layla: I was with C for years, and I craved someone to take care of me. He never stepped up to the plate, she says. She is now marrying a man her own age, of great wealth. He takes care of me, she says. I need that feeling of security. I adore him.

On some level, that feeling is ingrained, biologically. But on some level, with our new standing in the world, our own money, education, and freedom, I feel like we have come to the place men once held: I'm seeking a companion to my life, not for a life.

I met him that night—my birthday—at his house, where we sat by a large man-made lake in the early hours of dawn. His smell was terribly wild and brutal, yet warmly sweet, the scent of faraway fields and the smokiness of garam masala. He was at times, many times, an old man, older than me, conservative, formal. He didn't touch me, but once slid off my sandals and held my foot, on his knees. Madam, he said, your foot is very white. His hands holding it looked dark, casting off golden light. I laughed.

And then, suddenly, he sprang up, bouncing to a song dribbling from his car radio, and unabashedly danced, his unbuttoned oxford shirt wafting in the wind to reveal the sleeveless white tank clinging to his long, lean torso, without a trace of paunch or fat, and his loose, slouchy jeans, and I could see the college student, glaringly so, and felt at once excited and fearful: What am I doing?

After some time of meeting, chastely, finally the inevitable happened and we kissed.

He said, I will try and not kiss you.

And I said, that is best.

Meanwhile, his face was coming closer.

I will try not to.

You shouldn't.

I will try.

You—

But he did anyway, smashing his lips on mine.

This unleashed a miserable yet stunning series of events: a disheveling of clothes and honor and hearts. Literally, all walls fell aside, physical and mental.

After that, we were inseparable.

Those first weeks were a hazy time of nothingness. Never leaving the house, simply being together, eating dal and guacamole, the one dish he could make, ad nauseum. V, standing in his white tank and boxers, mixing guacamole with his hands is the image of that time.

The smell of incense, and his body.

I know what you want to know. And the answer is yes. A million times, yes!

I made him paneer, bhindi, kheer. He became my guinea pig for tasting my Indian food.

I could always tell if it worked or not.

I would give him my newest creation. If he was silent, not so good. If he loved it, he would slowly shake his head, and finally exclaim, shooting his hand in the air, UMMMMMM, MM, My God!

That was a success.

SARASVATI AND I never met again. We never talked again.

This left me with a great sense of sadness.

Suffice it to say, she did not approve.

Her recipes remain. And the sound of her voice in the background at times when I speak to him on the phone.

IT IS NOW two years later and I am writing this, and as I do a pot of kheer is cooking on the stove. I am jumping up to stir it every few minutes. It is for V, who is sick. He doesn't know I am cooking it. It will be a surprise.

He says I shouldn't be helping him. He will be OK. The usual half-hearted buffering from a sick person.

I remind him of how he came to me when I was sick and made maggi for me, the instant Indian noodles.

That large elephant is sleeping peacefully in a corner, satisfied, content, lying on a bed of straw.

SARA'S KHEER

- 1 liter of whole milk, preferably organic
- ¾ cup basmati rice
- ¼ cup dates, chopped
- 3 tablespoons almonds, slivered
- 3 tablespoons pistachios, chopped
- 3 tablespoons raisins
- ¼ teaspoon cardamom seeds, crushed
- A tiny pinch of saffron, crushed and melted in a tablespoon of milk (Optional)

Wash rice in a couple of rinses of water—5 times, to be exact—and soak for 20 minutes. Meanwhile, bring milk to a boil. When it comes to a boil, add drained rice and cook on low heat, until it thickens. This should take a full 50 minutes to an hour. It will start to thicken all at once and you must stir carefully as to not allow it to burn. Add the almonds and dates, pistachios and raisins. It is done when you lift a spoon and the rice has started to break down. Turn off the heat, remove and let cool. Now add sugar to taste. If you add it earlier during cooking it will burn or remain watery. Add saffron milk if you like the look and smell of saffron.

In fact, all the nuts and raisins are optional, too. You may wish just the pure cardamom flavor.

This is served warm or cold. Sara prefers it warm.

It is immensely soothing. It can rest a tired palate or soothe a sick person. It is also a prerequisite at a wedding or religious ceremony.

SARA'S BOTTLE GOURD KOFTAS (GHIA KOFTA)

Delicious, light, healthy! You can substitute zucchini.

KOFTAS:
* 1 pound bottle gourd or zucchini, peeled and grated
* ½ cup besan (chickpea flour)
* 1-inch piece of ginger, finely grated
* 1 clove garlic, finely chopped
* 1 teaspoon red chili powder
* 1 teaspoon amchoor (dried mango powder)
* 1 teaspoon coriander powder
* 1 teaspoon cumin powder
* 1 teaspoon garam masala
* 1 teaspoon ajwain seeds
* Salt to taste
* Vegetable oil for frying

GRAVY:
* 2 teaspoons oil plus 1 tablespoon ghee
* 2 onions, chopped
* 3 tomatoes, pureed
* 3 teaspoons coriander powder
* 2 teaspoons red chili powder
* 1 teaspoon turmeric powder
* 1 teaspoon garam masala
* ½ cup yogurt
* Salt to taste

FOR THE KOFTAS:

Combine all the ingredients in a bowl and mix well. It should be a thick paste; if not, add a bit more besan. Divide this mixture equally into walnut-sized balls and shape each into perfect rounds. Set aside.

Heat 3 inches of the oil in a kadhai (wok); carefully slide in the koftas one at a time. Fry until dark reddish-brown. Remove with a slotted spoon and drain the excess oil onto absorbent kitchen towels. Set aside.

FOR THE GRAVY:

Heat the oil plus ghee in a pan; add onion, garlic, and ginger. Fry until light brown. Add the tomato puree, coriander powder, red chili powder, turmeric powder, garam masala, and salt. Mix well. Add 2 cups water and bring the mixture to a boil. Boil uncovered until the gravy thickens. Add a small ladle of hot sauce to yogurt; stir. Then add to sauce. Add the fried koftas and cook for another 10 minutes on low heat. Serve hot.

SARA'S ALOO MATTAR WITH OKRA

An unusual combination. The okra falls apart and adds a silken texture, much like in gumbo. A nice one-pot meal with steamed basmati rice.

* 1½ cups peas
* 1 russet potato, peeled and cut in eight pieces, kept in a bowl of water
* 1 red onion, chopped
* 2 garlic cloves
* 2-inch piece of ginger, peeled and chopped
* 3 tomatoes, chopped
* 2 tablespoons oil
* 2 teaspoons coriander powder
* 1 teaspoon cumin powder
* ¼ teaspoon turmeric powder
* 1 teaspoon salt
* 1 teaspoon garam masala
* ½ teaspoon red chili powder
* 6 okra pods, each cut into fours
* 1 teaspoon sugar
* 2 tablespoons cilantro, chopped

Puree onions, ginger, tomato and garlic in food processor until thick, like a salsa. Heat oil in pressure cooker. When hot, sizzle cumin seeds. Add "salsa" mix and cook over medium-high heat for a good while—15 minutes—or until oil appears at edges. Add remaining spices, peas, okra, and potato. Add 2 cups water. Place top on pressure cooker and cook until one whistle. (It depends on your cooker and the ingredients, but maybe 10 minutes.) Then, turn down heat and let cook for another 5 minutes. Open after it has cooled down, let it sit for 5 minutes off the stove. Add sugar and cilantro.

SARA'S SOOJI HALWAH

Sooji is semolina, a medium-ground whole wheat. This dish has a very religious role, used as *prasad* (offering to Gods) in many auspicious days in India. It is very nutty and buttery, somewhat like toasted Cream of Wheat!

- 1 cup Sooji (or cream of wheat)
- 2 cups sugar
- 1 cup ghee (seems excessive but you will pour off much of it)
- 2 tablespoons dried assorted fruits (almonds, golden raisins)
- 3 cups of water
- A small pinch of saffron, crushed and dissolved in a tablespoon of warm water

Cook Sooji in ghee over medium-high heat until golden brown. It will take about 20 minutes. Keep stirring and watching. When brown, you may remove half the ghee with a spoon and save for a later use. Add dried fruits, sugar, and water. You may have to add a few more cups of water if it dries out. Cook on medium-high heat for another 20 minutes or until it resembles applesauce—thick and shiny. The oil should appear on the sides, indicating it is ready. Add saffron and serve warm (or ghee will congeal).

SARA'S PALAK PANEER

My ultimate favorite comfort food. This is the long version. See page 188 for the quick instant version.

- 1 bunch fresh organic spinach
- ¾ cup water
- 1 green chili, cut in half (serrano)
- 1 large red onion
- 1 large tomato
- 1 paneer, cut into 1-inch cubes
- 4 tablespoons oil
- 1-inch piece of ginger, cut in half, half of it cut into julienne
- 2 garlic cloves
- 4 cloves
- 2 teaspoons coriander powder
- 1 teaspoon cumin powder
- 1 teaspoon salt
- 1 teaspoon garam masala
- 1 teaspoon Kitchen King Masala
- ¼ cup heavy cream

Wash spinach thoroughly in several changes of water. No need to dry, just drain. Heat water to boiling point and add chili, ½ teaspoon salt, and spinach. Cook and wilt for about 5 minutes. Pour all into blender and carefully puree. Keep aside in blender.

Heat pan with 2 tablespoons of oil and lightly brown paneer on all sides. If you wish, you may omit this stage—the paneer will be softer and dissolve in the sauce more, which may be your taste.

Puree onion, garlic, and half of the ginger in a food processor until finely chopped. Heat remaining oil, and add cloves. Let this perfume for one minute, then add onion mix and cook for 10 minutes until the oil appears on the edges and the mix is golden. Add coriander powder, cumin powder, salt. Add spinach mix. (If the mix has thickened and you need a bit more water, rinse in the blender to dislodge the remaining spinach and pour in.) Stir and add garam masala and Kitchen King Masala. Add paneer, diced tomatoes, slivered ginger, and let cook for 10 minutes slowly. Add cream. Do not overcook, you will lose the emerald color.

Enjoy with chapathis.

Days of Shrines and Dosas

Light up the night, it is party time

*T*HE COOKING CONTINUES as does my affair with a taster, V, who more than happily will inform me of my progress as an Indian chef. I meet Suchita, who coincidentally lives in the same suburban enclave as V and Sara. When I drive there, my stomach feels slippery and odd driving by his house, as all endocrinal energy is directed there. But I drive on to her townhouse around the corner.

Suchita's house seems to be in a state of constant festival. It is a newly minted townhouse in a sparkling community of Route 50. Well-designed, with fountains, lakes, a splendidly appointed clubhouse, and pool. Driving up I somehow spot it immediately. Even though it is October, around the whole staircase she has draped Christmas lights, which I later learned was for Divali. The customary pile of shoes lie on her doorstep, and hers is a motley assortment of sparkly sandals, neon flip-flops and well-worn leather lace-ups. Inside, her husband, large and very dark with a beard, sits dutifully on the couch with a laptop, getting up to greet me woodenly.

Suchita is very young, twenty-something and curvy, a pretty rounded face with black eyes like starfish. Her house was brand new, with glossy furniture that stood out starkly, unadjusted to the space, blocky almost, and yet, the place was dirty simply from use—she had obviously cooked so many things in the last months, seemingly for hordes. There were rice kernels and carrot shavings lying dried in corners, and greasy stovetops, candy wrappers, and colorful lights, sparkling foils, and decorations still hung up crudely by Scotch tape. Yes, a good sign! Her small son had taken over a small corner room and this was crammed with every sort of bright injection-molded plastic toy ever made.

I ask her if she was having a party.

No, she laughs. We had Divali and all sorts of relatives here, and we never took down the lights. And then a birthday. And then Christmas and then more festivals, and we just never took it down. We just keep them up.

Divali is the Hindu festival of lights, celebrating the conquering of light over dark. Usually you have parties featuring lots of sweets and pujas (offerings) to Lakshmi, the goddess of wealth.

And that was the way with Suchita, whose name even sounded like Sweet. She had a soft and lackadaisical way of cooking, spilling spices and even burning things on occasion, but no worry, they tasted great. It is Suchita's wonderful dal I make several times a week, a rich mixture full of stewed chunks of tomato, and her methi (fenugreek) chapathis are delicious with a tiny of dollop of Mother's brand Tomato Pickle. Others favor ketchup or yogurt with chapathis, but I, like Suchita, really love the dollop of spicy pickle.

On my first visit, she insisted, along with showing me how to make that dal, on telling me what brands to buy. Only this garam masala, she said, it is the one which tastes like real Indian (though since I've perfected my own blend, see page 216). Only this brand of rice. Only this type of flour. And Suchita was right, certain brands really do cook better.

Suchita's dal is creamy and pink and absolutely delicious. I can live on this. It is simple and very healthy. Suchita told me the reason South

Indians are so smart (apparently this is a popular concept) is that they eat lots of seeds, which stimulate the brain. Dal is a lentil seed, of course.

She is very opinionated on everything. Rice, for example. In South India, we eat rice, she says. We are not bread eaters, like the North. And we prefer to eat Sona Masuri, which is light and very digestible, because it purportedly has less starch. In Telugu, Suchita's language, it is called Golden Ivy. Basmati rice is heavier, she says, and hard to digest (though gosh darned good, I think). Of course, I go and buy a large sack of Sona Masuri rice and start using it. I find it very nice, light, almost refreshing. It has its purpose; but I am still very fond of the perfumy basmati.

ONE DAY CAME the marriage conversation. I don't know how it started. I guess it's on my mind a lot. The more I wander into these homes, the more I feel like a disconnected raft wafting on the river of life. I wonder about the whole marriage thing. There are days when I fantasize about traveling the world, becoming a nomad of sorts when my children are in college. There are darker days when I truly think perhaps I should join an ashram and retreat from the world. And there are other days, too, when I fantasize about walking down a flower-lined path to an altar, surrounded by all my friends on a beautiful summer day and marrying a man who makes my heart cry. A man I truly love, a man who is a real partner to me, someone I actually choose. Someone to protect me in this world. I know that is so unfeminist, but something inside, I confess, longs for the strong man who will battle the world for me. If he could balance a checkbook, that would help as well. I point blank ask Suchita, Did you have an arranged marriage?

Oh no, she says, flipping a dosa, a super thin crispy pancake of rice flour from the south of India, that she is teaching me this day. Later, we will be making a coconut chutney to serve with it.

A love marriage?

Yes, in fact, we eloped . . .

She laughs sneakily.

He was my brother's friend, in his computer class. They would study together. I hung out with them, and—

She flipped the dosa, but it broke apart. We didn't care, it tasted delicious.

We fell in love. I told my parents and they said no. In fact, they had another choice for me set up. The marriage had been arranged and the date set.

Oh, so what did you do?

Well, what do you think? We came here and married here. It was quite a scandal for a while but now, they all accept.

Her husband always sat on the sofa, always on his computer and cell phone, often calling and scolding some third party. Obviously, there were major problems at his workplace and he was handling them from the couch:

I told you it wouldn't work. Did you call Mrs. Jane. Please call Mrs. Jane.

No, you will have to try the other program.

When you hear from Mrs. Jane, let me know.

He actually seemed rather gruff. There were no romantic sparks between them that I could see, no cooktchy-coos across the kitchen tables, but what did I know? Was I the expert of love and romance?

I come home with my containers full again, this time with Suchita's coconut chutney, a spicy and addictive dip you can slather on everything, and her wonderful dal.

And I light the incense.

And the candles.

And I look at Ganesh.

If you are born into my religion this would be viewed as idolatry. But the thought in Hinduism is that God, as he is referred to in the vedas, is *sat-chit-ananda vigraha,* or the form of complete spiritual essence, full of eternity, knowledge, and bliss, and is nonmaterial, completely nonphysical. His body, soul, form, qualities, names, etc., are all equally non-different. This form of God is not an idol designed from someone's imagination, but is the true form, as if God, this entirely indefinable substance, has descended into this material creation to hang out with us, so to speak. These are not products of the imagination, which would be idolatry. In other words, Ganesh or Krishna or Vishnu are actual incarnations or avatars of God's physical manifestations.

The purpose being so that one may actually experience God in a physical sense, since the true essence of God is beyond our senses or mind—vast and incomprehensible.

Ganesh is an avatar that explores wisdom and creation, amongst other things.

As I RESEARCH more stories about Ganesh, I learn coincidentally that tomorrow is the beginning of the ten-day-long celebration of Ganesh in India, specifically in Mumbai, where they will parade a huge statue of the God around the streets with much fanfare, and then finally throw it in the ocean. I make a note to attend this next year. But in the meantime, I do find a Hindu temple nearby that will be having a party and puja on Saturday, and I decide to attend. The website is colorful and says:

We worship that supreme power; Salutations to that Lord with a
bent trunk.

May that Lord with a tusk stimulate our creative faculties.

I'm not sure why I have singled out Ganesh or what he means.
But I intend to find out.

I end up not going. Do I just walk in? Too embarrassing. Next year,
I vow.

Meanwhile, my days are perfumed with the scents of coconut and
curry leaves. My nights, though, are sprinkled with kisses, the heavy fog
of incense in the air.

SUCHITA'S TOMATO DAL

This is my absolute favorite dal recipe and I make it twice a week, at least. It is fast due to the pressure cooker, which you *must* buy. It is the greatest thing ever.

- 1 cup toor dal (make sure it is not chana dal, they appear similar but are very different)
- 2 tomatoes, cut in rough chunks + ½ tomato diced for last-minute garnish
- ½ teaspoon turmeric powder
- 1½ teaspoons salt
- 3 tablespoons ghee or oil
- 1-inch piece of ginger, cut into slivers
- ½ small red onion, cut into slices
- 3 garlic cloves, crushed with a rolling pin and chopped
- ½ teaspoon mustard seeds
- ½ teaspoon cumin seeds
- 1 green chili, cut into rounds

Wash the dal several times in water, until it runs clear. Place in a pressure cooker with 1 cup of water, tomatoes, and turmeric. Cook for 3 whistles, then turn off and let cool for about 5 minutes. If you wish, you can release steam a bit here and there with the end of a knife. If you don't have a pressure cooker, you can cook the dal for about half an hour, until soft. Use a potato masher with the dal, adding the salt. Taste it and add more if you wish. Start a tadka with the ghee or oil in a small tadka pan, or small saucepan. Heat the oil until almost smoking on medium-high heat. Add the cumin seeds and mustard seeds and let it pop. Then add the rest of the ingredients, except the cilantro and extra tomato. Sizzle these items until they start to turn golden, drizzle them on the dal, stirring slightly (this is considered a garnish, and has a pleasant look). Add cilantro and diced tomato. Stir again lightly. Serve with rice, either sona masuri or basmati, or even chapathis.

SUCHITA'S DOSAS

These are crispy thin pancakes made of rice and lentil batter. Very nutritious, high in protein and no gluten! This is a basic recipe. You can fill it with cooked potato curry, for a delicious touch.

- A tawa, or a large flat pan
- 1 cup of rice
- ½ cup urad dal
- ½ teaspoon cumin powder
- ½ onion, sliced in half, skin left on
- 2–3 cups water

Wash and soak rice and dal together in 2 to 3 cups of water for at least 6 hours. Drain and grind them in a blender into a smooth batter. You may need to add a splash of water here and there for smooth grinding. It should resemble heavy whipping cream when done. Add cumin.

Put this in a large bowl and keep it in the oven overnight to ferment. In the morning, the batter will be doubled, usually. Add salt to the batter and stir thoroughly. Now the batter is ready for dosas.

Heat your large flat pan or griddle to medium-high. Much like pancakes, you really have to wait until it is thoroughly hot and you will probably mess up the first one. Drop a tiny bit of batter to see if it is done, it should splatter and sizzle immediately, yet not burn.

Dip the onion into a plate of oil and rub it all over the griddle. It is simply to temper the pan, an old traditional method. Now, take a ladle full of batter, pour in the middle and quickly, going concentrically, smooth out the batter to a large circle. It takes practice! It does not slide easily, it has to be pushed around with the bottom of the spoon in a circular way. Think of making a large spiral from the inside out. Mine are often not perfect circles, but most importantly spread the batter out so you have a thin pancake. Let cook for about two minutes. Sprinkle with a tiny bit of oil dipped onto a paper towel and flip over. Cook for another two minutes. The pancake should be crisp and golden. Serve flat or folded, with Sambar and coconut chutney.

SUCHITA'S COCONUT CHUTNEY

FOR THE COCONUT CHUTNEY:
- 1 cup fresh coconut, thinly sliced (or frozen or dried grated coconut)
- 3 small Indian green chilies, chopped (optional, you may wish for less, these will be hot)
- ¼ red onion, sliced into chunks
- 6 sprigs fresh cilantro
- 1-inch piece of ginger
- 2 tablespoons tamarind extract
- ¼ cup yogurt
- ¼ cup water
- 1 teaspoon salt
- 1 teaspoon sugar

FOR THE TADKA:
- 1 teaspoon each of mustard seeds, cumin, urad dal
- 2 fresh curry leaves
- A few pieces of dried red chili

First toast the onions in a pan at medium-high with a teaspoon of oil for about 5 minutes. In a blender, combine the remaining ingredients: coconut, onion, green chilies, cilantro, ginger, tamarind extract, salt, and sugar. Add water and yogurt and grind them until the ingredients are pureed. You may have to add a bit more water if it does not smooth out. The texture should be that of thick applesauce. Transfer the mixture to a bowl.

In a small pan, add ½ teaspoon of oil, add the tadka ingredients, sauté them until they start to splutter. Remove the pan from heat and add this to the pureed coconut mixture in the bowl. Taste for more salt. The chutney is ready.

SUCHITA'S PEANUT CHUTNEY

- 1 cup Indian peanuts
- 5 dried red chilies
- 1 small onion, sliced into big chunks
- 1 garlic clove, sliced into big chunks
- 2 teaspoons tamarind paste squeezed from pulp (see page 221)
- 1 cup water
- 2 tablespoons peanut oil
- 1 teaspoon salt or to taste

FOR THE TADKA:
- 1 teaspoon each cumin, mustard seeds, urad dal
- 6 curry leaves

Place an iron skillet on stovetop on medium heat. Slowly roast the peanuts to golden brown color. Cool and rub the skins off. This is a slow technique, but worth it. Indian peanuts have far better taste and you don't want the skins. You may buy unskinned peanuts and roast them in the oven on a sheet pan, at 350°F for 15 minutes, shaking the pan occasionally.

Heat 1 tablespoon of oil to smoking point in an iron skillet. Add and brown dried red chilies, onion, and garlic. This should take 10 minutes. Wait few minutes for them to cool down.

Put roasted peanuts in a blender or food processor. Grind to fine. Add other ingredients, plus tamarind, salt, and a cup of water. Grind entire mixture to fine consistency.

Remove the chutney to a bowl.

Heat 1 tablespoon oil in a small pan and sizzle tadka ingredients. Add them to the chutney. Mix and serve.

Whine Chicken

What to feed men

RAISING TWO BOYS can be unruly and trying at times, but mainly I have the sense that life is buckling along fast and I'm scampering behind. The house remains in a constant state of dishevelment, clothes and balls and backpacks strewn here and there. No matter how many times you pick them up, another pile magically appears. Socks seem to live permanently in hidden corners. As I visit the homes of their friends at the private school they attend, the houses seem so perfect and spotless, decorated with fillips of silk and tassels, while my single-mom household, living on a writer's small income—makes do with Ikea, used furniture, and shoes at the door.

But there is a buoyant sense of life to the chaos. There is laughter, humility, occasional slammed doors, hot foreheads tempered with cool washcloths, sleeping until noon, or whenever I pry these teenage boys out of their beds.

There have been, however, a few soothing salves for all life's woes through the years, simple and comfy recipes I devised years back that are able to bring this entire household back in balance. Now, of course, they are not complicated. One great hit was "wine chicken," basically a fine roast chicken cooked with wine, which is then steamed in its own juices, to impart the lusciousness of a roast chicken with the tenderness of a stew. But now that I am off meat, it is a bit of a problem. The recipe came from a mistake actually: I had to go to a baseball game so having bought a roast chicken, I covered it in foil at 200°F, and when I returned, it was magnificent. Now, as a foodie, I love to cook, and do it constantly, experimenting endlessly. There is no end to the dishes I have paraded in front of these boys—every form of Indian curry, stir-fry, and fritter; all sorts of Asian hotpots; exotic Middle Eastern stews with saffron and rosewater; sushi, and so on. And being children, they most certainly turned up their noses and asked for chicken fingers. And so, I created chicken fingers to end all chicken fingers. And homemade pizza, a surefire recipe. Pigs in a blanket, another.

But then came the fateful day Mom became a vegetarian.

What to do?

When the day is long and you are tired, and the kids are soon to jumble in the door in their cold-filled jackets, tracking in mud, cherry-cheeked, empty stomached, what can one make that will satisfy their hunger and my senses? A savory dish that will have them quietly "ahhh" as the smell hits their noses. There will be no whining, "what's for dinner," for they will know, as it heralds its appearance with the slow-cooked bugle of garlic and spices. A meal to calm all forms of young adolescent unruliness.

I am still experimenting on this. The comforting soups and curries don't sit as well with my boys.

However, my youngest is gathering a penchant for samosas with tamarind chutney.

He relishes a spicy chana chole with chapathis.

And the other day, desperately hungry, I fried him some parathas and served them with yogurt and tomato chutney, which he wolfed down.

As for the older one, he has been coaxed into enjoying paneer curry with pea pilaf.

Yes, it is very difficult to rear children in the midst of such awful food conditioning and expect them to have any sense of real, honest food anymore. Between school lunches and the bombardment of advertising, and peer pressure, they develop terrible tastes.

I think a simple approach is best: keep introducing new foods when they are hungry. Try new restaurants when they are starving. This has worked quite well for me.

My RELATIONSHIPS WITH the men in my life have been similar. Very quickly certain dishes of mine become their favorites, the standards of our time together. I think it is true of most relationships. The old adage "the way to man's heart is through the stomach" has been true in my case.

When I first met V, I made him dal. It was Stella's dal, the first I made back twenty-five years ago. I didn't know anything else, like chole or rajma or parathas, any of his favorites. But as he learned all the new things about America—our restaurants, music, women, schools, slang— and grew accustomed to the peaceful silence of Virginia as opposed to the bustling hodgepodge of Chandigarh where he grew up, I was learning the ancient foods of his land. Food his family had eaten for generations. I brought to him new foods: Mexican beans on tostadas, quesadillas, guacamole. Smoothies. American ice cream. Stuffed grape leaves. Hummus. All new vegetarian items he had never tried.

The first time he ate at my house, I forced a greens and feta pita sandwich in front of him. He cautiously ate it like he was four years old. He looked fearful, his eyes large and shining, chewing.

I found out he had never eaten anything in anyone's house, besides his own. He was afraid to, worried it would be non-vegetarian. In that moment he changed. Food brought him to a new world. He opened his eyes. My kids come bounding in the door looking for comfort. A man and a woman eat together as a bonding experience, an ancient rite of courtship. And sometimes, food is the gateway to a new life.

Spice, Spice Baby

A fiery lioness and her brood

I HAVE TO ADMIT I have a special feeling for the Punjabis. I find myself coming back to them again and again. Maybe it is destiny—my sister is married to a man from New Delhi, and my aunt is married to a Sikh. And I am in love with the mysterious V who is from Chandigarh. So, it must be in my blood, perhaps a past life returning and teasing me.

A woman named Jasmin popped up on my email. She exuded confidence and pluck. Immediately she declared herself a Punjabi and told me she was happy to teach me real Indian food, as opposed to the "crap" in restaurants. I knew I'd found a kindred soul—the food found in Indian restaurants is *nothing* like real, homemade Indian food and I really want my readers to taste the explosion of flavors that Indian food has to offer. The high-end restaurants have tended to tone down and deconstruct the real flavors of Indian cuisine, piling it vertically and pulling out chilies. The buffet Indian restaurants rely on cheap ingredients and mixes to charge little, and our palates suffer in the meantime. Not only that, cooking Indian food is an incredibly sensuous experience with the masala and the garlic, ginger and onions sautéing and filling the house with wonderful smokiness. It is very enriching for the soul.

V tells me the northern Indians are the best looking people in India, that the men are tall and "pulpy" and the women fair and tall. I've noticed again and again that the word "fair" or something similar is used to describe beauty in India parlance. Dark skin seems to be viewed as a disadvantage, which I think is unfortunate. I have pale skin, not white but pink, and freckled, and it seems so much less lovely than the golden glow of V's skin. He tells me, My whole family is pale. I am the only dark one, I look like a servant.

Punjabi food is known for its richness. They are great lovers of ghee, the clarified butter of India, drizzling it on everything. They are also bread-eaters, preferring paratha and chapathis to the ubiquitous rice of the South.

Jasmin, The Punjabi Princess, sums it up:

Punjab is the pride and jewel of India. Punjab is a very fertile land, and the home of the brave lions and lionesses. Punjab is primarily agrarian. When I think about Punjab, I can envision lehrate khet and mitti di khusboo. This means plush green pastures and the beautiful smell of the soil. In Punjab the winters are very very cold and the summers are very very hot. Punjab is, also, the home of the Sikhs. Golden Temple in Amritsar is the holiest gurudwara for the Sikhs all over the world. Punjabis are very friendly, fun loving, and warm blooded community. Punjabis are known for "khatardari," which means hospitality. Our most famous dish is Saag and Makki di Roti (Mustard vegetables and corn flatbread). Oh, don't forget to top it off with Lassi (yogurt drink). And the hand churned white butter is to die for. I have tasted it during my one rare visit to Punjab and I still remember it fondly. Nowhere in India will you find women more independent than in Punjab. Even today a woman driving a car is stared at in big cities like Delhi. In Punjab, it's so common to see women driving scooters in their salwar kameez and dupattas wrapped around their sides. It's an amazing site. I wasn't born in Punjab but the blood of Punjab runs through my veins. Punjabi spirit is wild and indestructible. Punjabi men and women are very good looking and hot. There is so much to say about Punjab that I wouldn't know when and where to stop.

JASMIN EXUDES ENERGY. She seems like the ancient warriors she talks about. She talks always of Punjabis and their reputation, and actually so does V. He says they are the beauties of India, that everyone knows that northerners are the lookers of India. Personally, I find there is lots of beauty everywhere, but I don't intrude on such nationalistic fervor. Northern Indian food is famous for its richness and delicacy of spicing, and I will say, it is warmly delicious.

We make an appointment. This woman is really different. She is powerful, intense. I am dying to know her.

We email back and forth for a while, arranging when to meet, etc.

Finally I come to her house and find a voluptuous and beautiful woman, with the classic Punjabi pale skin and dark hair, large pooling black eyes, shining with a devilish twinkle. Yes, she is spirited.

We are going to make Butter Chicken and Mattar Pulao (peas and rice). I don't have the heart to tell her that my book is vegetarian but she happily says it can be made with paneer as well, which is Paneer Mahkani, one of V's favorite dishes. I have tried to make it several times and found it difficult; there are too many versions online and they all contradict each other.

Her house is small and full of life, two scampery dogs bark and bark and have to be put inside the gate, and two moon-eyed, gorgeous boys, small and elfin, immediately bond with my large, gangly preteens and they all go off to play video games. And we start to make butter paneer.

Jasmin has a real passion for cooking: she tells me about the Punjabis and their love of butter. She tells me about *bhuna*, the act of roasting the spices, which I think is indeed the missing element in all my years of cooking those watery strews in my twenties. She has very particular ideas, as does everyone: No turmeric in spinach. No onions in the butter paneer. She adds her own touches, like paprika, for color (not an Indian spice), and honey, which really pulls together the spices.

And she tells me her story, in pieces.

I've had a really rough time, she says.

I was the daughter of a really strict Punjabi politician and I was wild. They didn't know what to do with me. I wanted to see the world, be free, go out! And I couldn't do anything!

I came here when I was fourteen.

You don't understand, I've lived on the streets, she says.

I can't pry. But, I come to understand that she was a typical teenager thrust into the teeming miasma of the U.S., with parents trying to restrict her to old Punjabi ways. It doesn't work very well, to say the least.

As a man I met named Dhruv tells me: You think you can come to the U.S. culture and pick and choose what you like or vice versa with India. You can't. It's a package deal.

I feel a certain closeness with her, but I also feel something I can't put my finger on. The sense of outsiderness. I feel it occasionally and it makes me feel, well, lonely. As if she hasn't figured me out yet. What am I talking about? This is the nature of life. We all mistrust each other, at first.

The thing is, these cooking classes become, at times, like auditioning for friends. And that is tiring. I have to remember that this is a professional arrangement, but I somehow start to care, and then I feel left out. And the other thing is, I often feel like an oddity, even as a writer, to everyone. A writer has a strange aura for people, as if you are doing something extraordinary and so you lose the everyday-ness with other friends. You stand off, alone.

And if there is one inner sensation that I know, I recognize, I am totally familiar with, it is that: Always standing away from the group, not fitting in. I wonder if I seek these situations out, the writing, the lessons, these are all ways of learning yet simultaneously standing apart from a group. It's a thought that gnaws on me.

Jasmin and I decide we will trade cooking lessons and she really wants to learn pasta. So, after some time, I invite her to my house. I am feeling guilty that I need to reciprocate her hospitality since she refused to take any money. She agrees to come one weekend, but then emails me that she is sick and has to cancel. That night, however, her Facebook entry leads me to believe she just had other plans and I feel sad. On some level, I think, I am kind of a novelty, the writer, a curiosity, coming in for a moment, and then, life goes on.

I try and put aside these feelings and concentrate on my mission: learning about Indian cooking, even though I am pulled in many directions, absorbing myself in the lives and cares of my two boys.

But Jasmin doesn't go away. She has a very nurturing side to her. She often emails and calls to see how I am doing. I sense we could be friends, beyond this cooking adventure.

I mark a day on my calendar where we can switch roles, where I can invite someone—like Jasmin—into my home and teach.

JASMIN'S BUTTER PANEER (SHAHI PANEER)

- 1 block of homemade paneer (you may brown it first lightly in some oil if you like)
- 5 cloves of garlic, chopped
- 1 red onion, cut up roughly
- 4 tomatoes, cut up roughly
- 4-inch chunk of ginger, chopped
- 1 stick of butter
- 5 cloves
- 1 stick cinnamon
- 2 teaspoons paprika
- 1 tablespoon tomato paste
- 1½ teaspoon garam masala
- 2 teaspoons salt
- ¼ teaspoon red chili powder
- 4 bay leaves
- 2 tablespoons honey
- 2 tablespoons dried methi (fenugreek)
- 1 cup heavy cream
- 2 tablespoons ground cashews

Puree the onion, tomato, ginger, and garlic in a food processor or blender until smooth-chunky, like a salsa. Heat butter in a pan, add cloves and cinnamon. When hot add "salsa" mixture. Cook this over medium-high heat for 15 minutes or until the oil appears around the sides. It is now time, as Jasmin said, for bhuna: to roast the spices. Add garam masala, salt, red chili powder, bay leaves, turmeric, tomato paste. Blend well and add honey. Add 1 cup of cream, methi, and stir well. Add cashews. Let cook for 5 minutes. Add some water if too thick. Add paneer and stir gently and let cook to absorb flavors on low for 7 minutes. Serve with Mattar Pulao, rotis, or chapathis.

JASMIN'S MATTAR PULAO

* 2 cups peas
* 4 cups basmati rice
* ½ cup oil
* 3 teaspoons cumin seeds
* 1½ cinnamon sticks
* 5 cloves
* 1 teaspoon paprika
* 1 teaspoon garam masala
* 3 teaspoons salt
* 7¼ cups water

Heat oil in a heavy deep pan. Sizzle cumin seeds until popping. Add whole garam masala and stir around to flavor oil. Add rice and cook a bit to harden the kernels in the oil, which prevents sticking. Then add all the rest of ingredients. Let boil for a while to absorb water, about 5 minutes. Then, cover top with a tea towel and a firm lid. Wrap ends of cloth up on lid. Let cook on low for 18 minutes. Let sit off heat for 5 minutes. Fluff and serve.

Saris and Saffron

A calm and serene Queen of Punjab

HEN I WALKED into Ujala's house, the smell of spices lingered down the hall. I think it must be incredible for her family to walk into this modern, gleaming apartment building, resplendent with marble entranceway and golden swirled lighting fixtures, modern geometric carpeting, and a game room with a pool table and huge wide-screen TV, in the created and attractive community of Reston; to walk through the halls and elevators of this building, after working and toiling, and to smell the wafting fragrance of ginger seared with cumin or the warm curtain of garam masala. These scents are the same scents their Punjabi ancestry has smelled through generations, dare I say thousands of years, whether they have lived in ancient mud huts or cinderblock or stone or simply wood and plastic.

This is what I love: I am trying to reinvigorate the concept of the hearth. Now, if I mention the word "hearth" to Americans, there will be an overwhelming cooing of pleasure—Oh, yes, I love a fireplace! Hearth, to Americans, equals a fireplace and in most cases in suburbia, my laboratory, a fireplace is gas-generated and rather sterile. No crackling wood, or smells. But it should be more than that: a hearth used to be the central focus of a house, for food, for altars and rituals, and for entertainment (storytelling), which is more than mere entertainment, for cultural bonding. It was essentially the zone of magic in ancient homes. The Latin word for hearth is "focus." It is the focus of a family.

The modern American woman views cooking as drudgery; this is a remnant from before our emancipation, when our only duties were child-rearing, guarding the hearth, and cooking. There is still a residual sense that cooking day in and day out is a prison. This then combines with the sense that there is no time for cooking, with most families consisting of two working members. But, there is time for television, many hours of it. TV is the modern equivalent of the hearth. Real cooking, involving your hands, chopping, touching, involving smell, has fallen to the wayside. Cooking has become a spectator sport, a fantasy on television with superstar chefs.

The sense of smell as a vital part of cooking is fading, and thus, so is taste, as they are intricately connected. The food we are cooking emanates less scent than before, which really disarms our pleasure receptors. In addition, much of our food is over processed, ill-farmed, altered so that the scent is diminished. In the past ten years, I've noticed a distinct lack of taste or smell in foods. For example, fresh basil, plucked from the garden, is overwhelmingly perfumed and herbal, creating a pesto that whips throughout your taste buds. Store bought hydroponic basil has the aromatic zing of iceberg lettuce. We are sadly losing the perfume of life, replacing it with artificially scented candles and wall plug-ins.

The average family in suburbia eats out three times a week. But one has to also account for the fact that most of what they are eating at home is not real, satisfying home prepared food—one has to look only at the change in grocery stores to know this—the meat department is slowly being taken over by packaged prepared dinners, frozen and fresh. The produce department is filling up with presliced vegetables and fruits. Sliced apples come in tiny packets for lunches. If we conceive of meals as tedious, they are not joy-filled. If you are invited to a home in middle- or upper-class suburbia in the U.S., you can expect to be greeted in a very lovely home with a kitchen that gleams. Upon the counter, you will find chips and dips of various assorted types, all store bought. Have you noticed how many new dips and sauces are available? After such an appetizer, dinner will be served: most likely a grilled fish or meat, because this is the domain of men and there is a reversal of power going on here—the man is adopting the cooking realm while the woman, to display emancipation, is eschewing food in general, in lieu of slimness and also, freedom. To accompany the meal, there may be bagged salad and bottled dressing. If I never see another pile of mesclun in my life, I would be happy. To that, there might be pasta with a bottled sauce. This is thought of as dinner party fare: but where is the cooking, the smells, the touch, the love?

TOUCH IS AN important element in the practice of Ayurveda: the consciousness of the cook affects the energy of the food prepared. It is well known in our culture that food cooked with "love" tastes better. It is said in India: "If you eat food prepared by the wicked, you will become wicked." This is important to remember in eating—at home or out—that the consciousness of the cook is in the food. How can the consciousness of a factory be good? It is thought that the consciousness of the animal or plant is available to us as well. Do you now see why spirituality and food are closely related? In Ayurveda, food preparation is considered holy. Therefore, one would want to choose products that have been achieved in the best circumstances—organic, lacking additives, preservatives, and pesticides. I don't want to proselytize on vegetarianism, but it is wise to consider that an animal has been killed, usually in a very high stress and terrifying environment, to give you sustenance.

The Indian homes that I have seen are utilitarian, basic. There is an unfurnished air, as if they are only here temporarily, on hold, and may dart off at any time. Perhaps this is the nature of northern Virginia, maybe companies transfer after a few years, so people feel no need to really settle in. Or maybe they plan to move back to India at one point. I cannot say and I realize my data is purely anecdotal. But I do notice it, each time I enter—a certain sparseness. The kitchen generally possesses a laboratory quality, a place where decoration doesn't occur but a serious task vital to the well-being of the family does. If they are vegetarian, this is even more so because it is very difficult to find wholesome vegetarian food on a consistent basis in this area. The vegetarian workers usually come home for lunch, if they can, or pack up their own. Therefore, it is vital that someone knows what they are doing, that someone takes it seriously. Most times in Indian homes, cooking is considered a female's duty, but realistically, and the women whispered this to me, sometimes the man is the one who does. And then, after many families, I realized many of them do cook. Frankly, what difference does it make? This book is not about placing American women back in their old roles, but about embracing cooking for the family and self as a spiritual and loving act benefitting all. If one is to have a solid family, someone should be making sure that healthy, home-prepared food is being served daily. Food is the cornerstone of memory, it stores the smells of our childhood. Nostalgia lives in the delight of the palate. By enjoying home-cooked meals together we are solidifying love, and bonding with our families, as well as caring about health.

As I said, the Indian kitchen is a laboratory—rather used-looking, greasy, not prettily arranged. Buckets of oil are handy as well as spatulas. Perhaps a spiral of chili sits in a corner or a mustard seed or two. I have come to recognize this slightly unkempt quality as a very good sign in anyone's kitchen. This is the sign of a real chef. Have you ever seen pictures of Julia Child's kitchen? All her tools on the coreboard wall set up like a handyman's garage. No fancy lavender tufts or ceramic rooster-topped jars. Likewise, when I enter a kitchen and see the state-of-the art granite and stainless steel appliances shining as if just bought yesterday, my heart sinks a bit: Here comes the mesclun, the Costco Vidalia Vinaigrette, the dry chicken breast branded by a grill.

BUT, BACK TO Ujala, who is as regal and calm as a queen yet still possesses the sweet face of a young girl. I enter her house—actually the small apartment of her daughter and son-in-law—and I am greeted most politely. I have come at 2:00 PM on a weekday, and am introduced to her husband, a solemn, polite man, and her attractive son-in-law. They offer me a seat on the one couch and we make very polite small talk. Ujala is a woman in her fifties, matronly, attractive in her gold and peach salwar kameez, with traditional gold jewelry, dark wavy hair, and a girlish shy smile. We awkwardly sit there chatting and then I am brought over to the kitchen, which is simply part of the room. It is fairly cluttered with a few pans, cookie jars, cereal, a yellow jar of ghee, soaking beans—again, the kitchen is used. If you walk into the studio of a painter, you would find it splashed with paint, brushes drying, jars of pigment assorted on the table. Or a sculptor's, such as my stepfather's, a studio chock-a-block with metal railings, planks, hardware, tools, rusty I-beams, etc. Or this writing office that I write in: papers in piles, a coffee cup, a candle, some incense, wires, pencils, books, clippings, tarot cards, a sprig of rosemary, a piece of driftwood—it reflects activity, usage. It is not making a statement except: this collage sums up a work in progress.

Ujala is from Delhi—here visiting for some time. She is going to teach me chole today. Now, I have learned chole already from Mishti from Gujarat in the North and from Meena of Pondicherry in the South. So, I am expecting the same. Cabinets are opened and shut, masalas pulled out. (I see one glass jar in the cabinet marked "backing soda." I notice it every time I come; it is innocent somehow and makes me smile.)

Slowly, as we cook, as we make bhature, the fried leavened breads, I realize that Ujala is a master; Ujala is the Queen of the Punjabis, the best cook of all. The chole, when done—when drizzled with ghee and frizzled green chilies and ginger slivers, plus chunks of potato—is mouthwateringly, stunningly delicious. I cannot even explain how it tasted, as if finally after my twenty-five years of searching, not knowing what it was only that it existed, I discovered the real taste of India. I sought it out. I found it.

Likewise, at the risk of seeming corny, I have found that love is the same. It is, at once, singular and convincingly itself, it needs no fussing or contriving. If I have learned one thing in my life, it is that: Love is simple, unerring, and very very strong. But there are many substitutes and many facsimiles along the way. The real substance, in any subject, is always effortlessly, pure and itself.

I COME TO Ujala's house and fall into the unutterable delight of her food, which is the ne plus ultra of anything. There is reverence and joy in her family for her art. For example, the last few times I went Ujala has told me proudly that her son-in-law's friends, all bachelors, will be coming over in the weekend for her chole. She beams. They will also, she adds, be playing poker. Probably all night. Cooking on the stove is a large pot of her chole in anticipation of the weekend event.

She also tells me how she pampers her family, how she wakes early to squeeze fresh orange juice for them and how, when they arrive at home, she blends strawberry milk. Her daughter not only works full-time but is going back to a local esteemed university for her master's. Her son-in-law is a hedge fund manager. They are a very ambitious, educated family, still living in the traditions of the past while straddling the future. This is done by sacrifice. Ujala and her husband are there to help them in this hectic time, the beginning of their marriage and their careers, by providing a safe haven of the "hearth," for the growth of their culture and bonding.

As vegetarians, it really is almost impossible for them to have nurturing food anywhere else. American offerings to vegetarians are salads, in general. Any restaurant will have a plain salad, maybe a vegetable plate, maybe hummus. One can't survive on this. The Indian rarely eats raw food, anyway, since they have a very distinct Eastern sense of "hot" and "cold" food, much like the Chinese. Salad, especially cucumbers, would be considered very cold. In winter, this would be dangerous as the only meal. One has to combine warm and cold foods very carefully. Not to mention, our personal temperaments. I tend to run "cold," therefore I prefer warming foods—ginger, garlic, cooked foods, to temper and ease my digestion. In order to survive in the U.S., a vegetarian must learn to cook at home. Ujala's children, without her presence, would be exhausted, and have little time to make these things. And yet, she will go back to India soon, after having spoiled them for a while. And then, they will turn to the pressure cooker for quick dal and simple things. Indian food is not so time consuming as one thinks once you develop a knack for it.

I'm coming back to my original thought, which is—in our modern era of two working adults—who is doing the cooking? I suppose there are several options. You could hire a cook, but you'd miss out on the therapeutic activity yourself. One person could stay at home and do all the domestic chores, which makes sense when you have small children and a reasonable income. Flexibility is key, because the workings of a family are not static and someone, preferably a parent, really should be with the children, rearing them. I am not advocating going back to the '50s. I am advocating a family that adjusts and balances in order to prioritize the children and the process and culture of a cuisine that nurtures them. And by no means am I saying you shouldn't eat out, just try to eat everything from scratch. I am saying, look at the process with new eyes. Realize that cooking a simple yet delicious meal, with quality ingredients, is incredibly therapeutic, bonding, sensually satisfying, and can be done together. It can be the glue of a family.

UJALA TELLS ME, as we make paneer, the delectable homemade cheese that is actually very easy, that this weekend she and her family will "be doing the picnic with tents." Oh, camping, I say. Yes, this one.

Interesting to imagine. We grab graham crackers, marshmallows and chocolate, maybe a few hot dogs.

But it is many things to bring for making the food, she adds with some trepidation.

I'll say. But then again, they diligently adhere to their tastes because, essentially, there is no choice. When they make a car trip, as they recently did to Niagara Falls, they pack up in Tiffins—puris (they travel well and keep at room temperature because they have a lot of oil), chole, dry vegetable curries, paneer, even dal. Which sounds wonderful, because on the East coast, the drive to New York has absolutely nothing to eat except fast food, Bob's Big Boy, and all that.

I have been going to Ujala's house for weeks and our conversation has always been very polite. I try and not pry, though I would love to know a lot of things. I would like to know what kind of Hindus they are and I guess I could ask, but Ujala has such a queenly presence, and I don't want to seem like some eager dog biting all over the place for tidbits of information.

In the center of the room they have a very beautiful altar, made of hammered and tooled metal in various designs, which holds a few small deities and flowers, and of course incense. I can see, when I peer over there, a small Durga prayer book.

Durga, I learn, is a mother goddess of protection. She has eighteen arms, wears red, and is seen riding a tiger. Her name means "fort" in Sanskrit or something difficult to overpower, and thus she is a protection against misery and evil. I also discover that she is an avatar of Parvati, who is the wife of Lord Shiva and the mother of Ganesh. There are, of course, thousands of different Gods and Goddesses in Hinduism, yet all are a form of Brahman, which is the great unknown, the ultimate. The three major Gods are Vishnu, Brahma, and Shiva, and you will find many avatars as well. It is all very confusing, but expressive of the many sides of our souls.

Think of Durga as a supreme warrior—riding on her Tiger, insurmountable, a friend in hard times.

In India, this great variety exists in the food as well. Thousands of varieties and variations. Hundreds of ways to cook cauliflower. Or dal. Or breads. Each time I learn one regional spectrum of dishes, I am invited into a home and introduced to an entirely new roster of foods, as well as a new language. I begin to see that this search will be a beginning, a small display of respect for such an abiding culture, and it will represent the dance that we Westerners and Easterners have done for centuries. At this point, with mutual respect, we must realize we have much to learn from each other.

And so I go on. I am very aware in these meetings, especially with Ujala and her family, that I somehow stand alone. I have no husband, and I both miss having a partner for my life, and revel in my freedom. I go day-to-day with mixed emotions. As much as I might love V I also cherish my space, my time. I delight in the long space of a day to write. I adore an unfilled weekend where the house is quiet, the kids are visiting their father. I light incense and sit at my desk all day long, unaware of time or space, awakening out of a fog around 4:00 PM, dazed, still in my pajamas, the house disheveled, the kitchen disorderly. When I emerge, late afternoon, my head is full with thoughts I have created. I walk the dog, have some tea. Slowly I come back to time and reality. Clean up, start a nice cooking of something in the kitchen, the house warms up, candles are lit. And then, perhaps V will come over and I will enjoy the presence of him so much, his wit, his charm. But had he been there during the day, I would have been angry and resentful, my desk calling, as I made breakfast for him. As much as he is young, he is also from another culture and still has old views of men and women: and I still cook. Sometimes I freak out and yell that he must do something. He does try, chopping tomatoes, making guacamole. But, still, it is still my domain. So I am all too aware that I am a by-product of this culture I live in—an extremely independent woman who needs space and time to create, who fends for herself, who earns for herself, yet is in love. But, I am simply not able to completely absorb into a partnership and give up that space. I teeter between both worlds, rather unsuccessfully I think, or maybe, with a slightly heavy heart.

Ujala tells me the story of how her daughter married this very "nice boy." She is proud of him, and rightly so. He is indeed respectful, has a good job, is handsome, kind, devout (despite the fact that I am there, he often comes in and prays in front of the hammered metal altar, his beads in his hand). Ujala says to me, I found him. Oh really, I perk up, my favorite subject. I envision a network from village to village, spreading the news of Ujala's daughter, sipping tea and evaluating, gossiping about the families, clucking, eating sweets, something from a Bollywood movie. But I am wrong.

I find him on Shaadi.com, she says. When I see him, I see he has very innocent face (he does, actually) and he is very good. I say that this is the one to my daughter. She also likes. But he says he must meet ten others. So, we do not hear. And I am thinking he is gone. But still I do not contact any other just in case he comes back. And then he does. We are very happy.

Shaadi.com is the new matchmaker on the corner, I realize. I ask others about it and learn that many people have used Shaadi.com, but I do not say so to Ujala. I go online and read the entries. One can find religious preference, region, language, age, horoscope, skin complexion (the traces of the caste system still quite prevalent), even caste directly. Oftentimes the ads are posted by aunts, mothers, sisters. The new dating network spans across to the U.S. and overseas. I saw postings from all over the world. Now from the comfort of one's own backyard one can learn cooking from someone across the globe in and find a suitable marriage partner. The world is open.

Ujala studied English in Shimla, in the foothills of the Himalayas, and then became married at twenty-one. Hers is the story of the old-fashioned network. Her aunt had a renter in Chandigarh who was a suitable bachelor, who asked her if she knew any good young ladies for marriage. The aunt said yes, and called Ujala's father. It was analyzed and decided. Then Ujala's family hosted a dinner for the man and they met.

Why was I sad this afternoon, as she told these stories while chilies fried and coriander powder fragranced the air? Why, after I just told you how I love my space? Because inside, on some level, as is the truth of us all, I want to belong with someone like this. Do I want to be matched without a word of my own thoughts, only to be hennaed and bejeweled and paraded up to an altar where a stranger sits, who will then make love to me that night, a man I have barely said hello to? It seems a great act of trust. No, I do not want that. But I do want to live out my life in love. And that is where I suppose we diverge. Westerners really idolize this idea of love. When it is gone, we divorce. They seem to think of marriage as a partnership; love is irrelevant, a lucky addition. Both ways are flawed. I sit on the fence, the modern woman, alone yet not alone, eating gobi fry on my own terms and going home to my house.

UJALA'S CHOLE BHATURE

You can use canned chickpeas if you prefer, but you are losing out on a particularly creamy texture that the dried ones, when cooked, retain.

- 1 cup dried kabali chana chickpeas (the normal golden variety found in the U.S., as opposed to kalichana, black chickpeas), soaked overnight in cold water plus ½ teaspoon baking soda, covering chickpeas by 2 inches (1 13-ounce can, drained, can be used instead)
- 2 small onions, or 1 large one
- 2 tomatoes
- 1–2 serrano chilies, depending on spiciness
- 2-inch piece of ginger, cut into small chunks
- 2 garlic cloves
- 1 teaspoon cumin seeds
- 4 cloves
- 1 teaspoon coriander powder
- ¼ teaspoon red chili powder (you can add more later when you determine how spicy the chilies are)
- 1 teaspoon cumin powder
- 1 teaspoon amchoor powder (dried mango powder)
- 4 teaspoons chole masala
- 2 tablespoons ghee
- 2 cups water

FOR THE DRIED CHICKPEAS:
Drain chickpeas and add to pressure cooker. Add water to cover by 2 inches plus ½ teaspoon salt. Put on high heat and after the first whistle remove immediately and allow to cool down for 5 minutes. Then loosen top carefully, open, and drain; allow to cool.

Place ginger, tomatoes, onions, and chilies into food processor. Puree until smooth, much like a salsa texture.

Heat a large Dutch oven or heavy pan on high heat. Add oil and when almost smoking, add cumin seeds and cloves. This will take only a second, the seeds will sizzle and start to turn brown, then immediately add the paste mixture. It will splatter like crazy—let it. Stir occasionally and let the mixture cook down. You may wish to turn it down to medium-high if your stove is so hot that it might burn. Stirring in the beginning seems to encourage the splattering, which is messy. This stage will take a good 10–15 minutes. It should be cooked down, be a warm orange color, and the oil should appear at the sides. Add coriander powder, chili powder, and 2 more teaspoons of oil. At this point, add the drained and cooked chickpeas (or drained canned chickpeas), and stir. Add chole masala and amchoor. Add water. Add 1 tablespoon of ghee. Cover. Let cook for 10 minutes. If you like it more soupy, add more water. It should be chestnut brown—add more chole masala if it is not.

FOR THE TADKA:
Dry potato chunks carefully. Heat deep oil in saucepan to 350°F. Add potato and cook for 10 minutes. Put aside and drain. Sprinkle with ½ teaspoon chaat masala, a sprinkle of red chili powder, and salt.

Heat ghee in a small saucepan, as small as possible. You can even use a stainless steel measuring cup (1 cup size). Add chilies and ginger slivers. Fry until golden. Put aside.

To serve: check chole for seasonings. It should be slightly tart, rich, and spicy. Place in bowl, top with potatoes, drizzle with tadka. Serve warm with bhature for scooping.

UJALA'S GOBI FRY (SPICED CAULIFLOWER)

This is bursting with flavor and considered a "dry" vegetable, without sauce. I am sure you will find it daunting—the cauliflower is deep fried in order to retain a beautiful golden color and custardy texture, but I have also roasted it in the oven with very good—and healthier—results.

- 1 large cauliflower, separated into large 2-inch florets, with small crisscross slices in the stem to enable cooking
- 1½ teaspoons cumin powder
- 1½ teaspoons coriander powder
- ½ teaspoon red chili powder
- ½ teaspoon turmeric powder
- 1 teaspoon salt
- ¼ teaspoon amchoor (dried mango powder)
- 2 tablespoons cilantro, chopped

Heat 2 cups of oil in deep saucepan until very hot (375°F). Add cauliflower and stir to cook on all sides and become caramel brown. This will take about 10 minutes. Drain on paper towels.

Alternatively, you may coat cauliflower in a spoon or two of oil, and bake in a preheated 400°F oven for 20 minutes, or until browned. After 10 minutes, flip the florets to brown the other side.

Heat 2 tablespoons of oil in a pan and add all dry spices. After 2 minutes of cooking, add cauliflower and coat. Cover and cook for 3 minutes in order to allow the spices to soak in. Serve on a plate sprinkled with cilantro.

UJALA'S PAU BHAJI

This is a famous street food in Mumbai, found on Chowpatty Beach, which has become a favorite dish all over India, kind of a comfort food and a weekend brunch food, as pancakes would be for Americans. It consists of a potato-vegetable puree, highly seasoned and buttery, served on a bun with raw onions and tomatoes. It was initially a fast lunch for mill workers in Mumbai.

- 1½ cups mattar, dried whole peas soaked overnight (the peas are optional but do add a nice amount of protein), cooked in 2 cups of water in pressure cooker to 1 whistle, and turned down to cook for 5 minutes on medium. Allow to cool.
- 2–3 Idaho potatoes, precooked in skin (Again, pressure cooker works well—cut in half, place in cooker with ¾ cup water, cook to 3 whistles, turn off. Or you may bake them.)
- 1½ cups green beans, cut into 1 inch pieces
- ½ cauliflower, cut into florets
- 1 cup green pepper, cut into medium chunks
- 1 large red onion, cut into chunks
- 7 Roma tomatoes, cut into fours
- 2-inch × 3-inch piece of ginger, cut into rough chunks
- 3 small green chilies
- 5 cloves of garlic
- 2 cups of peas
- ½ stick of butter

DRY SPICES:
- 3 teaspoons red chili powder
- 2 teaspoons coriander powder
- ½ teaspoon garam masala
- 2 teaspoons amchoor (dried mango powder)

- 8 teaspoons pau bhaji masala (use my recipe, or use Everest or Badshah brands)

Puree tomatoes, chilies, red onion, and garlic in food processor to resemble salsa. Drain mattar and set aside in a bowl. Put all vegetables, except potatoes, into pressure cooker and add 2 cups of water with 2 teaspoons of salt and ¼ teaspoon turmeric. After 1 whistle, turn down to simmer and cook for 5 minutes and place aside, with top still in place. You can also use a normal pan and cook for 20 minutes, or until very soft and mushy.

Place butter in pan on medium-high and add tomato mixture. Cook for 15–20 minutes until oil comes out around edges. To this add dry spices. Stir and add remaining butter. Taste for salt. Cook this for just 5 minutes more, otherwise you might burn the masala. You don't want this to brown, it should be orangey-red, or copper-colored.

Now drain vegetables, keeping the water. Mash vegetables, potatoes, and mattar with a masher into a rough puree. (Think of the consistency of a bowl of oatmeal.) You can use a hand blender here, though you don't want it to become like smooth yogurt. I have to tell you that my hostess added even more butter, probably another half a stick, which is optional. Again, this is not considered an everyday dish but a brunch or special weekend kind of thing, where you gorge and then relax the rest of the day. But it is delicious beyond words. Anyway, check for salt and make sure you have enough. It may require another teaspoon.

Place in a serving pan or bowl.

Melt *more* butter—4 tablespoons—in a pan on medium heat. Add ½ red chili powder. Drizzle on top. Place sliced onions and tomatoes on top and lemon wedges around sides.

Melt *more* butter in a pan on medium heat and toast each side of bread until golden. Serve pau bahji on a plate with a toasted roll and extra onion, tomato, and lemon.

Note: You don't need to add all this butter. But if you want authentic pau bhaji you do. Also, on some days you may have some leftover veggies. You can cook them further, add some of the mashed potatoes and tomato mix and have instant pau bhaji. Add a smidgeon of butter or none, and then you have a healthy week-day meal quite rapidly.

Or, you may just prefer to wait for the weekend, run a few miles, and drown in an orgiastic pau bhaji butter feast . . .

Enjoy, and then sleep for about three hours.

UJALA'S BESAN HALWA

This is a rich and creamy dessert made with chickpea flour, usually reserved for special parties, weddings and such. It is also a key devotional offering in Hinduism, like Sooji Halwah is, for Gods and Goddesses in puja ceremonies. It makes a very soothing dessert on a cold winter day.

- 1 cup besan (chickpea flour)
- 1 cup sugar
- 1 cup ghee (some of this will be poured off)
- 2 tablespoons dried fruits—almonds, golden raisins
- 3 cups water
- 1 cup milk
- A few strands of saffron, powdered with fingers or in mortar and pestle and melted in 2 tablespoons of hot water
- A pinch ground cardamom seed
- Slivered almonds for garnish

Cook besan in ghee over medium-high heat until golden brown. *Keep stirring* or it will burn. This will take about 15 minutes. After the besan has toasted, you can remove half the oil if you wish; it will simply pour off as the besan falls to the bottom. You can reuse the ghee for other dishes. Add the dried fruits, and stir for a few minutes. Add water, milk, sugar, and saffron water, and a pinch of cardamom.

Cook for 10 minutes. When it becomes thick, like applesauce, it will be ready. The oil, as usual, should show around the sides when the besan is cooked. When this is served, be sure and heat it to warm temperature, because the ghee will congeal. Garnish with slivered almonds.

UJALA'S JALFREZI PANEER

- 1 homemade block of paneer, cut into 1-inch pieces
- 1 yellow pepper, cut into large strips
- 1 red pepper, cut into large strips
- 1 green pepper, ditto
- 1 large red onion, cut in half and then into slices
- 1 tomato, cut into slices
- 1 cup fresh peas
- 2 green chilies, cut into rounds (optional)
- 2 tablespoons lemon juice
- 1 teaspoon sugar
- 1½ teaspoons salt
- 1½ teaspoons cumin powder
- 2 teaspoons paneer masala
- 1½ teaspoon garam masala

Heat a nonstick pan with 3 tablespoons of oil and brown paneer chunks on all sides until lightly golden. Place on a paper towel. Add another tablespoon of oil and sauté peppers and onions for 10 minutes. Add salt, cumin, peas, and chilies. Cook for another 9 minutes. Add tomatoes, both masala powders, paneer, and ½ teaspoon salt. Cook for 5 minutes. Add sugar, lemon juice. Stir well and cook for 1 minute to emulsify flavors. Serve with chapathis.

Diary of a Masala Junky

An aside about eating out . . .

I GREW UP IN a tiny town in Virginia called Delaplane. Actually, I can't even technically call it a town. With a population of perhaps fifty people, one train track, a faded yet charming country store with wheels of cheese and an old woodstove, and a post office offset by a few houses, it seemed to be more of an ancient outpost from the civil war. There were no restaurants in the town, but our neighboring town of Middleburg, a posh, horsey enclave, willingly treated us on occasions to what can only be called culinary experiments, meaning they had little success and faded rather quickly.

But my first restaurant memory was a bit more surreal and still to this day casts its warm glow: Before we lived in Delaplane my family lived in Washington DC and there existed one rather old-fashioned style brasserie, where, even at the young age of five, I indulged in Brains in Brown Butter and Crème Caramel, no doubt setting the course for my future zeal for all things written by Colette. But soon enough I was whisked away to the safe countryside of rolling meadows, thorough-bred horses, bourbon on the rocks, and a definite lack of restaurants. One local haunt was the family-run and cozy Coachstop restaurant in the middle of Middleburg. My then-divorced mother, my brother, and I would dine there on frequent weeknights on Salisbury steak with an ice cream scoop of mashed potatoes. There was not much competition: a small Rexall pharmacy with a counter served passable BLTs. In neighboring towns, the lack was the same: Although on one lone highway, there was a naughty steakhouse complete with a neon cocktail glass. I longed to go there then and still do now; people rumored the steak was good. But worse rumors came out through the years, one even my children now whisper: Once a child was abducted, they say, murdered, held captive in its basement. The mythology seems to get worse year after year. One of these days, damn it, I'm going to slip away over there and see for myself. I heard they have a decent olive and cheese plate, too.

There were other dining experiences I longed to discover. In the neighboring town of Winchester, a large town of 75,000, there existed Ruth's Tea Room, run by an elderly lady in her home. My father pointed it out to me once, just a simple house surrounded by trees. You had to call ahead. Ruth would treat guests to the most sublimely prepared steak. My father had been several times and said it was wonderful. Did she marinate it? A special sauce? He could never tell. There were no details. Just wonderful, he said. The years have gone and now Miss Ruth is dead. Her tea room closed, only a lovely memory.

Such is the charm of the small restaurant for a special few, no concern for profit or atmosphere, just lovingly prepared food. The Hindu religion believes that for food to contain the most healthful energy, it should be prepared by the clean hands of someone who cares for you. I imagine such warmth regarding Miss Ruth's Tea Room. I see her warm hands slicing bread, turning the steak with a fork over her enamel stove, while the soft laughter of folks rose from her living room outfitted with a few starched tablecloths she had ironed during the day.

Life continued on like this for some years, nibbling at the occasional diner we could find easily on the Virginia outskirts. And then, the '70s came.

Some local cognoscenti, hippyish types, opened a few new bold places. One local food goddess opened a swell French restaurant in an old colonial house in town, each room a tapestry of different colors. The excellently prepared French food was of the turn of the century. It was so suave: When you ordered iced tea it came with a tiny pitcher of sugar syrup. It was here, back before I became a vegetarian, I tried Duck a l'Orange and Pâté de Campagne. Down the street came a rather hip eatery called Cafe Le Rat. On my eighteenth birthday we celebrated with champagne and that tour de force of the '70s, a spinach salad prepared at the table, with bacon fried on site, crumbled over top, and a dressing made from the drippings.

But by the '80s, these ideas and restaurants had faded and we were left with boring places that served "meat, meat, and more meat," as a friend stated aptly, slabs of beef or pork, with little else besides a foil-wrapped potato.

In nearby Leesburg, a festive restaurant called the Hawaiian came to the town. My paternal grandfather, Frances, became a regular at their Trader Vic–like atmosphere of tikki lamps and great wicker thrones as chairs. He went every Wednesday. I tried it, sampled the pu pu platter. For Leesburg, it was an extravaganza, a thematic food festival. But, horrifyingly enough, after one year they were arrested for serving, yes, no urban myth, dog meat.

Nowadays in the countryside, the restaurant drought has been replaced and overrun, sadly, by upscale chains, serving food heated in plastic bags. Gone are the family run places, full of charm and incompetence.

The American suburban dining experience has become a shadow substitute for real culinary adventure. In a nearby town called Manassas, a pseudo crab shack imitates a windy, beachy seafood spot, complete with umbrellas. A Mexican eatery has artfully re-created the broken metal roofing and disintegrating wall plaster of a disheveled cantina in Mexico. Certain Italian chains bring us to a trattoria like that found in Tuscany, a sad substitute for many Americans who will never eat in an actual olive grove but can have a breadstick and a bowl of Minestrone and pretend to do so. The list goes on: A Floridian-style chain dressed in pastels and shutters offers conch and crab fritters; an Asian-themed grand-scale restaurant produces dumplings and chicken wrapped in lettuce. I'm not saying these aren't good—I go to them myself, in a certain mood of theatricality—but they are missing the hands-on approach of more intimate dining.

BACK IN MY small town, new options have sprung up. A passable French bistro, a few basic American dining places emphasizing a cluster of culinary oddities, overpriced and lacking the panache of the earlier '70s versions, the ones that seemed so ardently in love with new ideas, foods like pesto or Duck a l'Orange. Even those items seem stale to us now. These new restaurants utilize the flood of products, mainly culled overseas, that were once expensive and rare and now are affordable: tinned crab from Indonesia (instead of our excellent though dear Chesapeake Bay blue crab), farmed salmon, frozen tuna steaks and mussels. While they resemble our once favored items, they lack in flavor. The mussels steam with no particular odor, whereas in the past a pot of mussels would herald its arrival with its briny trumpet.

What seems to be lacking the most is simplicity: real fresh food cooked well.

But, fear not, if I wish to venture a bit further, half an hour or so, I can find delicious food places squeezed between the chains, small Vietnamese restaurants or Indian or pupusa shops. These places, family-run, simple, bring back food to its rightful place—delicious, real, wholesome. While the chains seem to emphasize atmosphere, the small places actually feature food. The urban sprawl, so despised by green urban planners, has one very delectable pay-off—a profusion of small mom and pop shops, without atmosphere completely, reeking of oil and fried spices, serving up fabulous regional foods of immigrants. There is the Eden center, a large shopping mall devoted to Vietnamese food, countless Korean Barbecue shops, mega grocers and a fantastic Sybaritic spa with a restaurant inside, an Indian shop in every strip mall, Russian groceries selling every form of garlicky sausage, Hispanic butchers, tacoria trucks, Ethiopian restaurants, Brazilian dried-meat shops, the list goes on and on, happily.

There is a small barbecue shop that my son has been insisting that we stop for along Route 50, an unassuming shack-like store, with a badly painted BBQ sign and a continuously smoking grill. Please mom, says my son, he learned barbecue in a cruise ship.

What?

We stop and I am not surprised in this cultural mishmash we live in to see a small, eager Punjabi man handling the whole thing.

Welcome, madam, he says. May I offer you a sample of my very fine, mesquite-grilled beef or pork rib? Also I am using applewood, you will not find a flavor to excel this one in any locale.

The man couldn't weigh more than 90 pounds, has sharp eyes in a face so bony he could have carved the cheekbones out with the large knife he is wielding. He's standing amidst pickled eggs and pork rinds in the old country shop.

His spiel continues, about marination, smoking, high-quality this and that, and I interrupt him: Tell me where you learned such food, please?—I'm just testing my son's story.

Madam, I was head barbecue chef on a famous cruise line for many years. I am now here as head chef, and the locals are starting to get wind. I have put my level best, waking at 4:00 AM and retiring at 11:00 PM, to produce the best barbecue the town can ever try. Last Saturday we were rock and rolling. We sold out.

Are you from Punjab? I ask.

Yes, I am, madam—how do you know this, please?

I can recognize your Northern features.

Ah, OK! You know tandoori then.

Yes.

Well, also in Punjab I was running a tandoor oven. Now I am here working like a dog all day long.

Are you getting profit sharing?

No ma'am. I am working for my green card. I don't even get minimum wage, ma'am.

I tell him that I am writing an Indian cookbook.

He becomes very interested. It occurs to me maybe he knows somebody good that will teach me.

Madam, you then know some Indian community?

Some, I say.

OK then, ma'am. Please. I am asking that you please try and find me one very good wife for me.

Punjabi?

Yes, madam.

What religion?

Sikh, ma'am.

He is very earnest.

Now I am a matchmaker, apparently.

Have you tried Shaadi.com?

Bhindi and Brown Eyes

Mimi

A CHANGE HAS HAPPENED: as I cook with Ujala, talk to Jasmin, and plan to meet a new lady named Mimi, from the South, a crisis occurs in my relationship with V.

On some level, we both knew that it would have to end sometime given the vast difference of our ages—the biological duties come into mind. While I have children and am content with the two wonderful ones I have, he would no doubt want to have children one day. The householding part of my life is coming to a close. I am coming into the later stage, where I hope to be a source of grounding for my kids, and for their kids, and to explore perhaps the latter stage of my life with travel and further writing. The days of late night nursing, diapers, and strollers are over. So there is a lingering sense of sadness in the fact that one day life itself will make us face decisions.

But, as it is, that happens harshly and fast. I get a call from him one day in the afternoon from the airport: He and his sister, Sara, are called back to India as his father was in a severe car accident. He may not survive the night. V is in the middle of his term, but as the only son, must return and care for them, his elderly parents, at this crisis. All the work and education, all his dreams, all of our moments and love, must be thrown away. This was his one chance in life to be educated in this country. In India, not being from a wealthy family and not getting into IIT, he has no future. He said at one point if he had to go back to India, he would start a brewery. I ponder that for some time.

But this is his nightmare. He has so many dreams. He wants to explore the world, become a hedge fund manager, open his own firm, give money to his family. And yet, he is returning to India. All of the sacrifices of his sister, paying for his education, his living expenses here in the States, seems to be for nothing. And further, there is the deep fear that his father will die. He and Sara are in the airport, stunned and tearful and afraid. It will be two days before they arrive back home in Chandigarh. Who knows what will happen then.

In the meantime, I guess the time has come for us to be over. At that moment, at the airport, we are over.

He doesn't say much, there is no use for big goodbyes or tears. He says just, I'll talk to you later.

Stunned, and confused, I stare out the window imagining him flying home, to palm trees and the insistent whine of nonstop Bollywood music. I have no way to call him or see him.

I have a fantasy of going to Chandigarh, staying in a nice hotel there, surprising him one day. I research it, price it out, and then sigh and forget about it.

I drift off into a dull fog.

I MEET WITH a woman named Mimi. I drive up to a large house and immediately see three brunette heads pop up from behind a fence in the backyard, all broadly smiling. They—Mimi, curvaceous, with a billow of dark hair, and two men, one quite handsome, and another with glasses, shy—greet me. They are working in her garden, and hidden behind Mimi is a tiny girl, just her beautiful dark eyes staring at me and then darting behind the soft comfort of her mother's knees.

I come to the back door and meet them all. It turns out that Mimi's husband is the shy one. The handsome one is a cousin visiting, looking for a job. They are all picking okra.

We go into the house.

Mimi tells me about her garden, and how she uses "square bed gardening," which uses a square wooden box, divided by grids, and plants set three inches apart. It's quite simple and useful, really, if you live in an urban environment. I go home afterwards and research it—it was developed by a man named Mel Bartholomew and he has a website, book, etc. Mimi's tiny garden is astounding, producing a huge store of vegetables in a small space. It is organic because she brought in new soil, did not use the soil in her backyard. She has okra, fenugreek, bitter melon, tomatoes, a green I do not know—called "Thotakura" in Telugu—all types of chilies, an endless smorgasbord. Most of her seeds were brought from India. Today she has harvested a large bowl of soft, velvety green okra that awaits cooking. Fresh methi, or fenugreek, lies in a pile.

Mimi tells me how she grew up on a farm outside in Andhra Pradesh, where her father used to have a large garden and how they grew up eating everything fresh from the garden. I understand this is not possible for everyone, but if every one of these suburban houses had a micro-garden, it would be life-changing. They would have instant organic food at their picking.

For lunch, she decides to make Bhindi Masala, or okra masala. She tells me she knows the secret of preventing the slimy quality in okra. Meanwhile, I am aware that a tiny creature is slinking down the stairs, and when I turn, the young girl cleverly twists herself around the banister, those two sparkling black eyes staring out.

She looks like V somehow, and I am saddened. Perhaps as a child he was a skinny little imp like this cute girl, with short hair that shimmered, and those eyes. I wonder what is happening with him. I don't even know if his father has died. I am in limbo, and starting to mourn the end of this thing, this indescribable relationship of no definition.

Mimi is cutting up the okra and I stand back and observe it all. I hear myself asking various food questions, how much for this, how much time, and then I help her crush garlic and ginger in a mortar and pestle, but my mind is far away—thinking why I haven't allowed myself to be part of a solid home anymore, where a couple lives and thrives together. Most of the Indian couples I have seen, and my own parents as well, tend to do their shopping together, on a Sunday or Saturday, as a huge outing. I see them at the grocer that I now frequent called Lotte in Chantilly, a huge, bustling Asian market that sells every form of exotic vegetable and spice, cooking woks and cleavers. It has noodle stalls, thousands of Korean pickles or Kimchi, a barber, a Chinese antique center, a seafood mart of gaping-eyed fish and scuttling crabs, and of course, an entire Indian section. Weekends will be thronging with sari-clad aunties in tow with the whole family amongst bustling Korean families, and me, drifting around, looking at dragon fruit and bitter melon, curry leaves and lychees.

I see couples buying their weekly food, huge bags of ginger and onions, garlic, heads of cauliflower. It is fun for me to look at everyone's carts and guess what they are making—Aloo Gobi, Palak Paneer, I can see the week's menu in display. But, sadly, if I go over to Wegman's, which I also frequent for cheeses and seafood, the carts display a completely opposite spectrum. Everything the Americans buy is largely premade and packaged. Truly. Yet another spectrum is Whole Foods, which represents a more urban, eclectic, educated crowd, following the mandates of a politically correct Dr. Weil, or Michael Pollan food approach. Their carts are full of organic food, high in anti-oxidants, perhaps vegan, or at least wild-caught salmon—food-derived vitamins and supplements. All fine, for sure, but horribly expensive. No wonder some people call it "Whole Paycheck." I adore shopping like this, but I am a single mom with two voracious sons and I have to budget.

But, while grinding the ginger-garlic paste, which has started to sharply fill the air, as the adorable little muffin has come closer and now runs to her mother's legs, it is the loneliness that I have chosen that saddens me. Here I find someone I can really connect to, but he is way too young and now, gone.

I blame myself on so many levels, and yet I know that any more of a relationship would have been too much for me. I like to devote myself 100 percent to my sons when they are with me. When I was engaged to the man before V, I always felt torn between him, his sons, and my own. I was the one who slaved over meals and cleaned up, while he sat on the couch. I felt my own sons getting lost somewhere in the crowd.

So I end up with nothing.

More crushing garlic.

And I wonder where V is. Why doesn't he even call?

And the little girl, who looks like V, has taken my heart. I feel sadder still that I couldn't have married him, had his children, that our times were not synchronized. It hurts.

Finally, I have finished the smashing and I realize that cooking is a wonderful form of meditation, that quietly using the tools of yesterday that don't save time but actually fill it, instills a pocket of time for reflection, an act which is being lost in our current speedy lifestyle. We have a desperate sense of needing to save time, but I wonder what we do with it? I imagine, quite honestly, that a lot of this extra time it is spent watching television or surfing the Internet.

Mimi and I make a delicious Aloo Gobi (cauliflower and potato curry). I have made these before, quite delectably, with Suchita, who flavored hers with mustard seed and turmeric, so I figured this would be the same, but no, it's quite different. This delightful version features copious amounts of ground ginger and garlic (thus my churning and yearning at the mortar and pestle) and a few handfuls of fresh methi leaves, which perfume the dish with a strong herbal scent. Dried methi is available in Indian markets and also quite good. Mimi packs me a small container of the wonderful dish and I leave, the rest of the afternoon laying open like a luscious gift, unplanned, sunny, sweet.

I go to get a pedicure. I small pleasure for sure, but something that helps me space out and relax. As I read the trashy magazines and bobble in the massage chair, my phone rings, I look down and see an odd number that stretches on forever, with too many zeroes and ones in front. It must be international:

India.

Nervous, hurt, confused, I let it ring. I am feeling vindictive, abandoned. My heart is rocketing in my chest.

I leave the shop. The warm food is beside me in the car.

The phone continues to ring.

And ring.

And ring.

Finally a voice message.

Nani. Please. I haven't much time. Please answer.

Finally, I pick up.

Thank God, he says.

MIMI'S ALOO GOBI METHI
(POTATO AND CAULIFLOWER CURRY, WITH FENUGREEK)

The fenugreek and dried mango add a tanginess.

- ½ head cauliflower, cut up into small ½-inch florets
- 4 russet potatoes, boiled, cooled, and peeled
- 3 tablespoons oil
- 4 cloves garlic
- 2-inch piece of ginger
- 2 teaspoons coriander powder
- 2 teaspoons jeera seeds (cumin)
- 1½ teaspoons salt
- ½ teaspoon red chili powder
- 1½ teaspoons chaat masala
- 1½ teaspoons amchoor (dried mango powder)
- ½ teaspoon garam masala
- ½ cup methi (fenugreek)

Mash ginger and garlic in a mortar and pestle (or grind in a food processor) until pureed roughly. Mash potato with hands into rough chunks. Put pan on high heat, add oil and let heat up. Add cumin seed. Add garlic-ginger paste and let cook for 5 minutes. Add chopped cauliflower, both masala mixtures, ½ cup water. Cover and cook until soft on medium heat for 10 minutes. Uncover, cook until water is gone. Add potatoes, methi, and a touch more oil to make it crispy. Serve warm with breads. This is a dry curry.

MIMI'S NAVARATNA KURMA, OR NINE JEWELS
(NINE TYPES OF VEGETABLES COOKED IN A CASHEW SAUCE)

A sumptuous, festive dish that looks very creamy but is completely vegan and high in protein.

- 6 small red potatoes, cut into fours
- 1 cup small cauliflower florets
- ½ cup green beans, sliced into four pieces
- ½ cup carrots, cut into 1-inch chunks
- ½ cup peas
- ½ cup corn
- ½ cup tomatoes, chopped
- 2 cups red onions, chopped
- 2 cups raw unsalted cashews
- 5 cloves garlic
- 4-inch piece of ginger
- 2–3 green serrano chilies
- 8 tablespoons canola oil
- 3 bay leaves
- 5 cloves
- 3 cardamom pods
- ½ cinnamon stick
- ¾ cup golden raisins
- ½ teaspoon shah jeera (black cumin seeds)
- ½ cup cashews
- 1 cup almonds, chopped
- 1 cup water

Boil cashews and onions together for 10 minutes, until soft. Put aside to cool. Boil all the vegetables in salted water until soft, for 20–25 minutes. You could steam as well, but the vegetables should be soft and not lose their color. Meanwhile, grind ginger and garlic to a paste in food processor or mortar and pestle, which is how I learned to do it and it does make it much more flavorful. Blend cashew mix in blender until very white and smooth.

Heat a deep pan on medium-high heat. Add oil. When heated add: bay leaves, cloves, cardamom pods (lightly crushed open), cinnamon, shah jeera, garlic and ginger paste. Let brown for 10 minutes and add cashew sauce. Stir well. Add chilies. Cook until all water evaporates and oil appears on edges. Add salt. Add cashews, almonds, raisins, and well-drained vegetables. Sprinkle with garam masala. Let simmer for 10 minutes. Serve with white rice.

MIMI'S CABBAGE AND COCONUT RICE

- 2 cups green cabbage, finely chopped
- ½ cup red onion, finely chopped
- 3 tablespoons oil (1½ + 1½)
- 1 teaspoon urad dal
- 1 teaspoon raw white sesame seeds
- 1 teaspoon coriander seeds
- 3 tablespoons fresh grated coconut or dried
- 2 red chilies (Mimi used 4–5, your choice)
- 1 teaspoon ginger, chopped
- ¾ cup water (¼ cup + ½ cup)

Cook plain steamed basmati rice. Put aside and let cool.

Heat 1½ tablespoons oil in a pan for spice mixture: add urad dal, sesame seeds, coriander seeds, coconut, and red chilies. Toast well. Add spice mixture along with ginger to a blender. Add ¼ cup water and blend to a white paste.

Heat 1½ tablespoons oil in a wide pan. Sizzle mustard seeds and curry leaves. Add cabbage, onions, spice mix, and ½ cup water. Cover for 10 minutes, stirring occasionally. Toss with cooked rice and taste for salt.

MIMI'S BHINDI MASALA

- 1 pound of okra
- 2 red onions, chopped
- 2 tomatoes, chopped
- 2 tablespoons oil, more if needed
- ½ teaspoon turmeric powder
- 1 teaspoon coriander powder
- 1 teaspoon cumin powder
- ½ teaspoon chili powder
- 1 teaspoon salt
- ½ teaspoon amchoor (dried mango powder) or 1 teaspoon lime juice
- 1 teaspoon garam masala

Rinse okra, remove ends, and cut into four pieces lengthwise. Put 2 tablespoons oil in pan on medium-high heat and cook onions until soft, for about 10 minutes. Add the four spices and salt. Add okra and stir to coat. You may need to add more oil; do not add water as it will become slimy. Cover and cook on medium-high heat. About 6 minutes later, stir and add tomatoes and cover again for another 6 minutes. Uncover and add amchoor and garam masala. Serve with nan, chapathis, or rice.

Spices, with Benefits

Living in a pressure cooker. Living with a pressure cooker

NANI, I CAN'T begin to tell you how it has been, the misery I have seen, he begins.

It is almost summer and it is beginning to rain. I want to rush home before it really gets going, but it is too late and the rain beats on the car in great sweeping gray sheets and I have to pull over. Blanketed by this wet torrent in the car, Mimi's food is still warm next to me on the seat.

It's raining here, I say.

It's always raining here, he says. That is when you should have chai and pakoras.

I soften. I will try and make Mishti's pakoras.

I would have called you but I was in the hospital. You don't understand. There is no room for my father. He is in agony waiting for surgery. He is on a cot in the hall, and I am sleeping under him.

How does someone understand such a thing, that this could exist? It is hard to pull my head around it. He sleeps under the bed?

I'm in the critical care unit, it is, it's, I can't explain. A family came in yesterday, screaming that their daughter was sick, she couldn't breathe, she was like, fourteen, and then she coughed and blood came out, and she died right there and those people started screeching, hitting themselves, yelling, but this—

He was quiet, I could hear a lot of men speaking Hindi in the back and interference crackling along the phone lines.

This, this is always happening. Nani, I—

I didn't know how to help him. Me, just eating food, feeling sorry for myself.

Why can't he get surgery? I had a million questions, thoughts, answers but they seemed to just annoy, they came down to questions of prestige and money. I felt helpless.

His father wouldn't take medicine. And the doctors were too busy. It seemed that every simple task, like getting an ambulance, involved paying large amounts of money. There seemed to be other issues as well, secrecy, not wanting prying neighbors to know. Or distant family members. That they might come, complain, and take away their money, he said. You don't know India, he told me. People might gossip and destroy their standing. Many incomprehensible things that seemed unreal.

The Hindi in the background got louder and he stopped and yelled back at the men.

What did you say?

I told them to shut up, I'm speaking to U.S.

There was silence now.

Where are you, anyway?

I'm in a phone shop. I have to get back to wash him. I have to do all the work, washing him. But I'm going to call my teachers so I can still study.

THUS BEGAN THE summer of phone calls from a small phone shop in Chandigarh, India, with a background chatter of two men in Hindi, while I started testing the recipes I had learned so far.

Chopping garlic and ginger, I would cradle the phone and hear a voice far away, seven hour time zone difference, tell me how he would wash his own father three times a day to prevent infection because the nurses were too busy. And how his father, in pain, threatened to leave this earth on a daily basis, perhaps he was also suffering from depression. It seemed that since he hadn't had surgery immediately, his bones started to grow misshapen. He begged to die, V told me.

Some nights, V said, he would say to me "game over." Game over, meaning he would die. I would lie under the bed and just wait. Finally, when I would come up again, he was still breathing, just sleeping. Then, the emergencies would start grinding in the door—bleedings, infections, all kinds of cries and screams as people literally died in front of you. Do you get it? V would say, his voice crazed: I'm studying economics and people are dying on the floor!

I would never get it, not really, though I tried.

Powerless, my only way to feel close to him was to cook.

While I was stirring in coriander and cumin powder, grinding a fumy garam masala, he would tell me how he studied all night under the cot, and was preparing to still take his exams.

I stuffed bhindi with coconut and rolled chapathis again and again with my new wooden roller, while he spoke of death and dying on the other side of the world.

The schedule was reversed because of the time difference, so my nights were spent talking to poor V, who slowly was losing the grasp on his dreams. His father needed him more and more.

The surgery never happened and his father's bones repaired incorrectly, misshapen. Finally, his father came home to recover, which was almost worse, because now V had the whole family to support and manage, amidst the chaos of pain and grief. He had to rent out an old apartment because they had just moved to a new house and the old house was empty and could bring in revenue. He had to fix the electricity when it went out, which was frequently. Or the computer, which jammed all the time and was slow. If we Skyped or chatted, it was often cut off.

I'd say what happened, and he'd answer, Nani, you don't understand. It's India.

He became more and more reclusive, tending his father, who I could hear yelling sometimes in the background, and then retreating to his room, eating parathas and yogurt, while I, in the States, ironically learned to roll them and fry them.

It was a connection to him in some small way.

At least we ate the same food.

Summer came and the raw Virginia heat sizzled on the black pavement. In Chandigarh, I could hear the pelting rain through the phone. His voice crackled as he talked about his days, rubbing turmeric on his father's wounds, cleaning him still three times a day. His voice was weak and it took very little to set him off, yelling at me for nothing, and if I hung up, he would call back over and over, until weary, I would pick up. Once he called 162 times. I couldn't abandon him, I would always pick up eventually, yet I felt like I was trapped in a very small dark tunnel.

I wondered if this would go on forever. Me, testing Indian recipes, talking to India.

Sometimes I bought phone cards from the local Indian shop, where I bought spices and a Ganesh statue.

I prayed to Ganesh to help V and his family.

Then suddenly, just over a month when he left so suddenly, he was coming back.

He was running through the airport, with big bags and smelling of old sandalwood powder and the sour smell of airplane travel wafting as we hugged.

BACK AT HIS house, V appeared thinner and darker, with large black circles under his beautiful eyes. Like an ancient merchant back from the seven seas, he pulled out gift after gift—sequined red dresses, boxes of bangles, earrings and necklaces, scarves, embroidered shawls, prints of Indian court princesses, and one more thing, wrapped in a tissue, a box:

A pressure cooker. The Indian ones are much better and I had longed for one.

As a present, I will make him some Mattar Paneer, his favorite dish that I make.

He is also really fond of vegetable biryani that I have been making lately.

You are the best friend I ever had, he said, kissing me against the wall. I missed you desperately.

I remember it was raining that summer afternoon, darkening the house. We stayed in the bed for hours in a sweet embrace and then woke later, the rain still beating the roof.

When it rains, Indians eat pakoras and tea. I put aside the plans for mattar paneer and biryani, and just made pakoras.

Soon the house was full of the spicy smell of chai and pakoras. I made cauliflower, potato, spinach, and paneer.

We sat and ate them in silence, watching the rain, while in Chandigarh it also rained.

MISHTI'S PAKORAS

- 1 cup besan (chickpea flour), more if needed
- 1 teaspoon red chili
- Salt
- Cold water, up to 1 cup
- 2 teaspoons garam masala
- 1 tablespoon ginger, grated
- ½ cauliflower, cut into 1-inch florets
- 1 potato, cut into 2-inch x ½-inch sticks
- 1 block of paneer, cut into 2-inch blocks
- 2 cups chopped raw spinach

Heat oil to 360°F.

Mix 1 cup besan with chili, 1 teaspoon garam masala, and ginger. Add water, stirring to create a thick batter but not too thick—something like pancake batter. Add salt. Take the blocks of paneer, slice through the middle into two thin slices. Salt and sprinkle garam masala on one side and cover with another slice, like a sandwich. Do this to all pieces.

Start cooking cauliflower—dip in batter with hand and slide in oil gently. It should rise after a second and start browning. If it sinks, wait for oil to heat further. Do the same with potato and when brown, place on a towel-covered plate to drain. Carefully dip paneer "sandwiches" in batter and fry.

When everything is done, refry potatoes and cauliflower, as they tend to cook longer.

Mix chopped spinach in separate bowl with ½ teaspoon salt and ½ teaspoon garam masala. Add besan and mix with hands, squeezing until it becomes a thick paste, like mashed potatoes. Drop by large spoonfuls in oil for fritters.

Serve with tamarind chutney and mint-coriander chutney.

UJALA'S PANEER MASALA

- 2 blocks paneer, cut into 1-inch squares
- 2 red onions, chopped
- 2 tablespoons oil
- 1½ teaspoons turmeric powder
- 2 teaspoons coriander powder
- 1 teaspoon cumin powder
- 1 teaspoon salt
- 2 teaspoons paneer masala mixture
- 2 tomatoes, sliced
- 2 large pinches methi
- 2 tablespoons butter
- 2 tablespoons sour cream

Heat oil in pan and lightly brown paneer. Drain on paper towels.

Heat 2 tablespoons oil and fry onions over high heat, add rest of ingredients and simmer. Add paneer and methi. Serve warm with rice.

The Keralan Sea and Fresh Coconuts

In the temple of love

THOUGH V SETTLED back in, his father never fully recovered, lying in his bed in their new house in Chandigarh, becoming an invalid. He couldn't urinate and so a catheter had to be used, and it became infected frequently. There were long calls to India for V, after which he would glumly sit, feeling shameful and guilty for not being there and helping his mother and sister, and confused because ultimately the only way he really could help them was by continuing his education so that he could provide for them one day. It became clear to me and to him that his father was in a great depression, yet he would never consider medication for this.

Summer in Virginia is hot. But not as hot as Kerela, says a woman named Beena, who lives down Route 50 about twenty minutes from my house. She is a small ball of energy, and she wears a long braid down her back. She opens the door for me and a curtain of curry leaf steam, oakishly metallic, billows from the door. I'm making chutney, she informs me.

Slipping off my sandals and putting them with the heaps of others, I come into another spare house with a large smiling family, a mother, a father, several small children asking and interrupting for ice cream.

No, later, she tells them, and they run off to the other room to watch TV.

It is now Beena and her mother in the kitchen.

The little girl comes in again.

Mama, I want it though, she says.

OK, girl, the grandmother says, getting up, tell you what.

Sipping chai, which such hospitable people always generously give me, I watch the grandmother with her long, skinny gray braid.

Everyone's chai is different, a special home recipe. For theirs they slice large hunks of ginger. Sara grated ginger into hers. Mishti liked lots of cardamom, and so forth.

The grandma then slices a mango for the girl into a glass bowl.

I want to kill my daughter, she gives this one everything, she says, and Beena laughs.

There are small signs of Christianity in the house, which is prevalent in Kerala. Small plaques that hold tidbits of the scriptures. A cross.

Kerala is a very special place, says Beena. We miss it a lot.

This house is very grand. It is decorated and beautiful. Two large brass elephants adorn the dining room table. So even though Ganesh is not here, at least I don't see him, these other elephants herald his presence.

I SOON DISCOVER it is indeed a special place. The state of Kerala in India has a population of twenty-nine million, yet astoundingly boasts a literacy rate of 100 percent. There are other anomalies, too—the average life expectancy is seventy-two, while ours is seventy, yet this is a very poor state in India. The average family has two children, lower than 60 percent of other poor countries in the world. V tells me that southerners are considered the smart ones in India. Beena tells me as well. It is because we eat so many seeds, she says, this is brain food, implying pulses and the like.

Meanwhile, however, the grand occasion called Ganesha Chaturthi, the birthday of Ganesh, is coming and I really want to go.

I am embarrassed to ask anyone, without seeming too prying. This is not something V would go to since he is a Radhasoami. So once again I go to Craigslist. I post an ad in the community asking for someone to please take me to the festival. I am flooded with responses, again.

After much going back and forth with various people, a large percentage of whom are married men and seem to want an easy opportunity to slide into a convenient encounter, one man seems genuine, funny. R says he doesn't like religion, that it is the cause of the world's problems, but he is Hindu and could take me to a temple. It turns out he is from Kerala as well.

Why do I trust him, you may ask? It just seems to me he has a peaceful nature. He sends me a picture of a hawk-eyed man with a long ponytail in front of a beach.

We meet in a parking lot of a very fashionable outdoor mall, where singles love to come and eat dinner in the overcrowded chain restaurants. He drives up in a shiny, brand-new black Mustang GT, which he is very proud of. He tells me everything he knows about Ganesh. But most importantly for him, he tells me about the food at temples and what to expect.

The real reason, he says, is he wants to go eat some vadas.

That is acceptable, I tell him.

On the way over, we listen to heavy metal on satellite radio.

He asks me if I want to go to a KISS concert, which I politely decline.

He says his favorite band is Guns N' Roses.

Finally we arrive at the temple, which astounds me. It is a giant rectangle of corrugated metal sheeting and cheap plywood. A wooden ramp leads to a very basic front door. It looks like a storage unit for farming equipment. There are just a few cars there—I expected a massive crowd. After reading about the Ganesha Chaturthi in Mumbai, which attracts an amazing ten million followers every year, I am surprised to see three cars.

I hope they still have vadas, he says.

We walk in, take our shoes off, and suddenly we are in a vestibule, with small handwritten signs for food and "offerings"—one can pay extra to have the priest make special blessings for you. We then enter the main hall, and I catch my breath, literally. There are huge statues of Ganesh on a raised area, like a stage, and the place is very small and intimate. Each statue is festooned with garlands of flowers, necklaces of pearls, and jewels. There are piles of offerings—bananas and sweets in front of the God. Incense fills the air and a few families are sitting, chanting.

It is stunningly lovely.

I am a bit embarrassed to be the only non-Indian here, but no one seems to mind, in fact, they all smile warmly. We sit on reed mats, people praying around us quietly.

R whispers, I think we might have missed it. Should we go?

I say, well, let me stay a few minutes and experience this.

There are so many sights that I have never seen. I need to take it all in. I see there are a few side tables used for holding items. They must have been simple plastic tables that they wrapped in tin foil to appear more fancy. I see various odd dusting items—fluffy gray fur or feathers jutting from an engraved silver holder. I ask R what they are. He says he thinks they are fancy dusting thingies.

He loves this word "thingy" and uses it to describe everything.

Just when we are about to leave, a man comes through and tells us that the priest will be performing the ritual again in about ten minutes. I can see that R is not very eager and literally deflates a bit. But we sit and wait.

Suddenly, a man with long black hair comes bounding out, wrapped in what appears to be a sari-like long piece of gold-trimmed fabric. He is half-naked, which is rather surprising if you were raised Christian, where the minister or priest is quite covered. I read later that this is so he is naked in front of God. I can see his unadorned brown back, with his long black ponytail. He has a very jolly face and smiles at me kindly, immediately taking the dusters and using them to whisk them in a ritualistic way over the statues, whilst reciting prayers. I can hear the words Sri Ganapati and also Lakshmi occasionally, but that is all I know. He lights some oil and performs various rituals at the altar.

Next, he comes to us, bringing a lamp that everyone gathers around to wave the smoke towards oneself. I believe this is for Lakshmi. The man has us grace our foreheads with a red powder dot, using our ring finger. He pours ginger water into our hands and we drink it. Lastly, after many prayers and mantras, he gives us each a small token of nuts and raisins to eat. Actually, he runs out of these in the middle and goes and finds a large economy size plastic container full of the stuff from Costco, and dumps it into the sacred bowl.

Afterwards, much to R's deep dissatisfaction, they are out of vadas. We had come a bit late. So, instead, we have lemon rice, which is delicious on its own—light, crunchy and very tart. It makes a great picnic food. We sit outside with a family on a picnic bench and eat it.

They study us and one rather curious woman asks me: Oh, are you colleagues?

And I say, No, we are friends. And then I can see more questions in the woman's eyes.

When we drive home, R tells me about his motorcycle. How he lives in a new apartment complex called "The Reserve," right next to the fancy mall where we met. He likes to drive his motorcycle over to the bars there sometimes and hang out. He told me that last week he met a woman there who asked where he lived, and when he said "The Reserve," she said, I didn't know there was an Indian reservation around here. We laugh as he drops me off.

It is interesting that I come back to Kerala, which is where this cooking started in the first place, in Brooklyn, cooking with Stella, who made the best dal, parathas, green curries and chutneys, dosas and idlis. I have since lost track of her, it has been fifteen years. I know she is back there, in Kerala.

I asked her once why she didn't marry again. She was a sweet woman and very pretty.

She snorted slightly. My husband beat me, she said. That was all she said on the matter.

One day, I want to go to Kerala and stay there. Maybe I will see Stella.

R asks me if I wanted to go for coffee. I say no. I wish I could tell him that it is not personal, but I don't bother. The summer with V has been tumultuous and strange, up and down. It has left me feeling unsatisfied, sad, but worst of all, it has turned my heart off from other men. I simply feel no interest.

IN JULY I had gone to a writer's colony in upstate New York. I found, after some time, that the women there talked less about work and projects, and more about men and dating, and about when they would get married or have a kid. I had this overwhelming feeling—since I hear many unmarried thirty- and forty-somethings, my demographic, obsessively discussing these things—that we still have the old values we've always had. Maybe biology is destiny. All I know is that all the choices we have assist us intellectually, ideologically, but I'm not so sure about emotionally. Women of this era are the result of too many choices and conflicting feelings. We want to fall in love, yet to be independent. We want a career and a family and no sacrifices. But what ends up often happening is a woman hasn't made a choice and finds her fertility running out, or a couple juggles too many things and has to send their kids to daycare. Quality relationships require some form of sacrifice, and I didn't think we wanted that anymore. So, not strangely, many forty-somethings are going with younger men. We want no commitments, fun, something energetic and beautiful—an accompaniment to our lives, not a main course. The thought of falling in love with a man with his own kids and household and merging those fills me with dread of a giant chaos-filled life of constant excursions and loudness. These days, I have the boisterous life of kids when I am with them. When they go to their father's house, I often need a sun-lit room with incense and total quiet for writing. The younger man is flexible, likes to try new things, is OK with your space and your ways. He comes and goes.

But then, conflictedly, I harbor a pit of swirling loneliness inside where I seem to crave a man that would somehow guard me against the brutalities of the harsh world, and I think probably most women do. It is ingrained and animal. This sensation causes us to long for the romantic surrender.

How nice it would be not to be the one who wakes at 6:00 AM and packs the car for a long trip, as my husband used to do, or when I make dinner, he could take the kids out somewhere. Instead I am grappling with all these duties, plus all the bills, by myself.

But in my life, I have a young man who is in the midst of family turmoil, and also applying to transfer out of the community college and into a good school. Despite the long hours under a hospital bed doing his work, and amidst the hours of caretaking of his father and family, V made it onto the dean's list. We struggle with how we will feel. I believe I will now walk alone and so will he, though he hates it when I try and talk about this. So, we don't.

Like every other woman I know, I do not know what I want. I will want one thing and then, I will change my mind.

How simple it used to be when a woman just wanted a husband.

At the writing colony, I learned the men were different. They wanted women for sure, but they were not pinning their whole destinies on it. A woman would accompany their lives, not define it. A very engaging man at the colony, gay, older, the life of the party, interrupts this endless conversation I am having with a girl who not only writes poems but plays professional poker. She also is searching for the Right One, through a sea of men that just don't interest her. She has too many choices, too many ideas.

Girls, he says to us. This is what my therapist says: You get two choices. The rest you have to accept.

We mull on this.

For me, he says, it's come down to Soulful and Submissive.

We laugh. I like "soulful." But what about Kind, Intelligent, Educated, Successful, Handsome, Funny?

As usual, we have a long list.

I think on this. I'm STILL thinking on this. Afraid one choice will veto another.

It reminds me of my friend Brinda.

We met at a writer's conference and became fast friends. One day we decided to go to Kripalu, a yoga retreat in Massachusetts for a yoga–hiking weekend.

Driving up from the city, I told her we would be doing a soul-mate ritual I had read about.

She was cynical. Are you crazy? she said.

Yes, I said. What have we got to lose?

Again, I have no scruples against anything supernatural or magical, as long as it is not damaging to others. I read that in witchcraft, one does not do love spells for one specific person, because this is called "caging" and you are messing with someone's consciousness. Am I a witch? No. Do I believe in these things? Absolutely I believe that there is much more to life than we can possibly know, and I respect this. I am, as I have said, not atheist or agnostic. I am spiritual, non-exclusionist. I am a seeker. As an artist, I would love to know all the forms of artistic expression that exist. Who knows what I might learn that might assist my own vision? I may not like it all, but I want to know about it all. I do not say "this is wrong" or "this isn't valid." I accept and learn.

So the first step in the ritual was to write a letter to each other describing the perfect traits of our soul mate. As in "Dear Brinda, I have met my perfect soul mate, he is . . . blah blah blah." We are supposed to be as detailed as possible. So much so that to this day I tease her about one part: "must love fine fabrics"—is that really important, Brin? Must love brocade, satin, crepe de chine? Are you hiring a designer or seeking a life partner?

This was years ago. We did the ritual. She ended up just a few months later driving across the country to California and got caught in an ice storm in Arkansas and literally all traffic had to be waylaid at a truck stop. She stayed there overnight to wait it out with a bunch of truckers in a diner, talking all night with heavy mugs of coffee, hashing out their lives during this odd act of God, whilst the roads outside glistened in clear, smooth sheets of ice.

One man in particular seemed to "get" her. He reminded her of her father. He seemed warm and thoughtful.

I felt like I knew him, she said. I haven't felt like that before.

Well, do you have his address or number? I asked.

No.

Oh, well.

I forgot, she forgot. But three weeks later, she called me.

He called, she said out of breath. He researched my company and found me.

Wow.

He's coming up this weekend.

Two months later, they were married and she moved down to Texas.

This is where we women go. We can't resist the fairy tale. We want the prince to rescue us, we can't seem to get out of this part of ourselves.

And anyway. When she went to Texas, she found out he lived next door to his mom. They were born-again Christians. He told her to leave her gay friends and her New York liberal life behind. He watched John Wayne movies.

And me? I fell in love with a sexy Indian boy-man, half sage meditator, half texting, hiphop-loving, an odd mix for a forty-something non-cougar writer who likes to write and cook.

Brinda left him, incidentally, of course.

We're going to Kripalu again in two months.

I'm going to bring some paper in the car.

So, I SAID no to R for coffee because of my heart. The heart just acts its own way and does what it wants. I can't go out because I love someone, whatever that might mean. I am definitely in unchartered territory. A place foreign and unreal, much like Kerala.

A week later R sends me a recipe from Kerala, which I sample and find very good. The recipe comes to me like this, which charms me, almost like an e. e. cummings poem, full of life and love. I change it to vegetarian and it is quite delicious.

now 4 the biryani u need, meat 250 gm rice 150 gm onion 150 gm jeeragam 1 tsp pepper 14 tsp coriander powder 1 tsp chili powder 14 tsp turmeric powder 14 tsp garlic paste 14 tsp ginger paste 14 tsp milk 50 ml ghee or oil 75 ml curd 14 cup coriander leaves 2–4 (chopped) mint leaves 2–4 (chopped) green chilies 2 lime juice 1 tsp cinnamon 1 very small piece clove 2 cardamom 1 salt to taste.

grind jerakam, pepper, coriander, chili & turmeric powders, green chilies, cinnamon, cardamom & clove. mix this paste with curd, chopped coriander & mint leaves, lime juice & meat. keep aside for 30 minutes. fry in ghee 34 onion till brown & crispy remove & in the same oil cook the meat with rest of the onion 14 fried onion. u can add water if needed. cook till water evaporates & a thick gravy is left behind. cook rice as usual with salt. u can cook rice in a rice cooker. remove this. in the rice cooker put a layer of meat & gravy, fried onions kissmiss & cashew nut (these 2 things i forgot 2 mention earlier) & then a layer of rice. repeat till rice & gravy are finished. sprinkle milk & switch on the cooker. it will go off automatically when the rice is cooked. before eating mix the contents well. thats all u have to do 4 making biryani. try this weekend & tell me how it came.

love,
amma

My response was such:

Do you have a recipe for banana curry?

HE SENT ME one for banana curry and one for mooru curry. Both delicious.

As for Beena, it was over before it started. She may have been my best teacher, I will never know. She lived so far, forty minutes away, that I couldn't find the time. I told her and she disappeared into that vast wide world of ours, never to show up again. Sometimes I think of her, randomly, no reason. I suppose this is how we live as well, as small snapshots in other's hearts and minds. I think of the two brass elephants on her table. Like a dream, they seem symbolic and I carry them with me.

BANANA CURRY

A very quick and luscious curry.

- 2 bananas, not too ripe
- ½ green pepper, cut into ½ inch squares
- 1 red onion, diced
- 1 medium sweet potato, peeled and diced into 1-inch cubes
- 1 teaspoon black mustard seeds
- 1 teaspoon whole cumin seeds
- 2 dried red chilies
- 2 fresh curry leaves (optional)
- 1 teaspoon ground coriander powder
- 1 teaspoon ground cumin
- 1 tablespoon grated ginger
- 1 chopped garlic clove
- 2 teaspoons sugar
- 1 teaspoon salt
- 1 can coconut milk
- 2 tablespoons tamarind puree
- 2 tablespoons canola oil

Heat oil in pan on medium high heat; add mustard and cumin seeds and allow to sputter. Add red chilies and allow to roast for 30 seconds. Add curry leaves. Add green peppers and onion and fry for five minutes. Add ginger, garlic, sugar, salt, coconut milk, sweet potato, 1 banana sliced into the pot, and 1 cup water. Cook for 20 minutes on medium heat, or until sweet potato is soft but not mushy. The banana will have disintegrated. Stir and add tamarind puree and the remaining banana, also sliced into the pot. Serve over steamed white rice.

BEENA'S COCONUT DAL (PARIPPU)

- 1 cup toor dal
- 3 green chilies, slit lengthwise
- ½ teaspoon red chili powder
- 2 garlic cloves
- ½ teaspoon cumin seeds
- 1 red onion, chopped
- ¼ teaspoon turmeric powder
- ½ cup coconut, grated
- 1 tablespoon coconut oil
- 1 tablespoon ghee
- ½ teaspoon mustard seeds
- 2 teaspoons red onion, minced
- 2 red chilies, broken into 4 pieces
- 3 curry leaves

Heat oil and add cumin seeds. Cook onions until soft, about 10 minutes. Add coconut, turmeric, garlic, and mix in food processor until a thick paste.

Pressure cook dal for three whistles and let cool down. Mix in the green chilies and bring to a boil. Add the ground ingredients next and bring again to a boil. It will be thick as batter now. Heat coconut oil and ghee, add the tadka ingredients (mustard seeds, minced red onion, red chilies, and curry leaves), and let them fry and darken. Pour the tadka over the dal.

Serve hot with rice, chapathis.

CHITRANNAM (LEMON RICE)

This is an amazing burst of flavors and textures: citrusy, crunchy, and bright yellow due to the turmeric. An excellent room temperature summer dish.

- 4 cups of freshly cooked Sona Masuri rice, though basmati is fine as well
- ½ cup fresh squeezed lime or lemon juice
- 5 green serrano chilies (or Thai Bird chilies, if you want it truly South Indian hot)
- 2 tablespoons urad dal (white lentils)
- 2 tablespoons ghee
- ½ teaspoon cumin seeds
- 1 teaspoon mustard seeds
- 2 dried red chilies, broken into thirds
- 15 fresh curry leaves
- 1 teaspoon turmeric powder
- 1 teaspoon salt
- ½ cup cashews
- ½ cup skinless unroasted peanuts

In a heavy pan, add half the ghee and fry peanuts and cashews until golden. Put aside.

Add remaining ghee and let heat until the oil is hot and separating in the pan. Sizzle curry leaves, followed by the cumin and mustard seeds. Next, add the split green chilies and urad dal and fry until golden and crisp. Add the turmeric powder.

Add all ingredients to a large bowl, including rice, spices, and citrus juice. Toss lightly with a wooden spoon. Taste. The flavor should be quite lemony; add more citrus juice if needed. Serve with yogurt.

Viennese Days, Gujarati Nights

Be careful what you pray for

I KEEP GETTING EMAILS from a gentleman from Gujarat. I ignore him because I do not want to go to a man's house, just as a safety matter. I have gotten lots of replies from college students who say, *ya I cn teach u my ma's dal*, and such, hoping to pick up some easy cash or I don't know, maybe hoping for more in the bargain, so I just avoid any of that. I have had some serious conversations with a wine sommelier who admits he can't cook but has given me a lot of advice on wine pairing with Indian food.

But in general, I tend to prefer to learn with Indian women. But the Gujarati man insists and then says, he is inquiring for his mother. She is in town for his wedding for a few months and wishes to teach me.

I have mentioned how much I love Gujarati food. This is considered by many to be the best vegetarian Indian food there is. And also, it is lighter and fresher than the classic moghul-influenced food of the North. And I discovered with Mishti, they like it sweet! They add sugar to everything. Someone told me it is because the natural tap water is slightly sour and this counters it. I do not know, but I know that it is delicious.

The Gujarati man, named Chandran, tells me he is planning to get married. He says that maybe afterwards is the best time, right now they are very busy.

Secretly, I really wish they would invite me. I've never been to an Indian wedding. My sister had a traditional Hindu wedding but it was in New Delhi. And my aunt, who married a Sikh, had a Western wedding. I've actually only gone to one international wedding ever and that was Afghani. And it was amazing. It was a huge affair, the most overdone thing I have ever seen. Everyone wore evening gowns and tuxedos. There was a table absolutely cascading with fruits and pastries, and on the food buffet, a baby lamb under heat lamps. Most visually stunning was the bride—sitting on a stage in a fluffy antebellum lace gown the jarring blue of car antifreeze, complete with a bright blue veil. The groom was dark and handsome, with the peculiar pencil-thin sideburns of a '90s boy band. Actually, looking around, I noticed all the young men sported this look. There was a large procession of presents, all stacked upon one another like towers, much like the style of stacked gift boxes one can find in a Harry & David store around Christmas time. The guests—family, I assume—came dancing in to music, holding the gifts. Yes, that is right, they had to dance in a procession with the gifts and bestow them at the feet of the betrothed until the huge, glittering potlatch of gifts hid the couple. Then, there was a very elaborate ceremony of gift-giving by the groom to the bride, boxes of jewelry opened as she sat there.

During dinner I learned that this was only an engagement party. And the girl was only sixteen. All of this took place in a fairly mediocre Sheraton, with brass and patterned carpets, in Alexandria, Virginia.

So my fantasy was to go to an Indian wedding as well. I know the customs—my favorite being that the groom rides up on a white horse. But I daren't ask Chandran. And anyway, as it turns out, they are finished with the wedding by the time they invite me to their house. I put aside that dream for now.

DURING THIS TIME, I have been studying the Ayurvedic properties of food. I have read several books, and endless websites about the subject, discovering that many foods have medicinal properties that make them beneficial for health. Turmeric, for example, is one of the most powerful antioxidants in existence. In Ayurveda, it is considered a vital purifier of the body, a healer of wounds—remember I told you V would put this on his father's wounds—an antiseptic and antibacterial, a liver strengthener. Ujala had told me if my body ached to drink turmeric with milk at night.

When I come to Chandran's house, a simple townhouse in Vienna, I am graciously greeted by his mother, Jayaben, in full sari. She is a diminutive lady with a classic long braid, diamond nose earring, and matching diamond earrings. We sit and chat for some time. Indian people are so gracious to me in this process, and their hospitality has been really amazing. I am given a glass of water, not chai. How funny.

Then after a bit, I am led to the table. There has been much talk about the new wife, who is not there. I suspect that is because they do not know her very well. Apparently she is an ABCD (American Born Confused Desi), though Chandran was born in India. And she just married, and is now living with an only son and his mother. What a combustible situation for an American! I can't imagine how this would work. Most women I know would be apt to bolt. If it doesn't work out, we can get our own place, we have possibilities, and are taught to think for ourselves. This woman, being an ABCD, would no doubt have that same mentality. Caught between both worlds, I imagine it is quite hard.

We are waiting for her to arrive before we eat: When she does come in, I am surprised by her manners. She rather gruffly greets me, complaining that she is tired and hungry. I get up and shake her left hand, because she is holding a computer and books with the other. And anyway, I am the one who reached out, not her. She does so out of duty. She plops her stuff down on the couch and ignores me completely—not that I expected to be worshipped, but she really could care less.

The husband seems to tiptoe around her, as if she is a tinderbox about to blow.

We are sitting at the table awaiting her. She says she'll come "in some time."

Chandran nervously giggles.

I wonder if I am the problem. Maybe she doesn't want a stranger in the house.

Finally she joins us. The table is set with many small bowls of yummy looking things I have never seen before. Tiny bowls of grains and mixtures. I am most excited.

First, Jayaben gives me a glass of cold buttermilk with cumin.

In Gujarat, says Chandran, there is a classic worker's meal—just a glass of buttermilk, a whole onion eaten like an apple, and a generous serving of Bajra Na Rotla—a thick, dense roti made from millet flour. Very delicious, with an almost earthy flavor of buckwheat.

Next, I notice other bowls—a raw grated beet salad, a dry fry of sprouted mung beans, dal, a porridge-like mix of roasted eggplant, pickles, and a tiny bowl of bright orange carrot slivers—

Carrot?

They taste sharp, pungent, herbaceous—they are actually delicious slivers of fresh turmeric root, seasoned with lemon juice and salt. Vivid is what I would call them; the root jolts through your body, a saffron-hued partner of ginger.

The wife is now calling her husband "sweetheart" at every chance. I am racing with confusion. Something feels off here and I can't figure out what it is. I conclude—after the baffling meal, after she says how great "Mom's" sweets are—and yes, they are, we delight in a delicious walnut-date fudge—that this is a family readjusting and reinventing itself. This is a new marriage and it feels, well, awkward right now, but after time, since this is how it is done, hopefully it will smooth out.

These people are Vaishnavas, the branch of Hinduism that follows Krishna, they tell me. Just like Mishti, who was also from Gujarat. They talked of their temple as we eat the splendid meal. Chandran had told me when he first emailed that I should just come and taste his mother's food and there would be no charge, and then we would discuss schedules. I thought this quite generous and kind of them—and was delighted by the food.

But when I returned home and emailed them, thanking them and saying how much I loved it, Chandran told me that Mom decided it would not be worth her time, that in order to do it I would need to pay her double the fee and bring my own food and supplies. I felt very hurt, and on some weird level, rather mislead. I countered that I could bring the food and increased the price a bit, but explained that I had posted my price and that I had other teachers as well. It really was starting to add up! Sadly, we did not end up working together.

HAUNTED BY THE food Jayaben had cooked, I emailed Mishti and she sent me recipes and I worked on them. Especially I was enchanted by the turmeric. I went to an Asian grocery and found a bin of the bright, neon roots. They look like small, skinny ginger roots and when you break them open, they are the most gorgeous neon saffron hue. I recommend eating a few slivers every day.

The health properties of turmeric are amazing:

Turmeric has properties as an alterative, analgesic, antibacterial, anti-inflammatory, antitumor, anti-allergic, antioxidant, antiseptic, antispasmodic, astringent, cardiovascular, carminative, cholagogue, digestive, diuretic, stimulant, and vulnerary.

It is known to assist in helping anemia, cancer, diabetes, digestion, food poisoning, gallstones, indigestion, IBS, parasites, poor circulation, staph infections, and wounds.

Turmeric helps to regulate the female reproductive system and purifies the uterus and breast milk, and in men it purifies and builds semen.

It reduces fevers, diarrhea, urinary disorders, insanity, poisoning, cough, and lactation problems in general. Turmeric is used to treat external ulcers that respond to nothing else. Turmeric decreases kapha (the two elements water and earth) and so is used to remove mucus in the throat, watery discharges like leucorrhoea, and any pus in the eyes, ears, or in wounds, etc. I've even read that a poultice of turmeric is used to treat lepers.

One note in cooking: A study conducted in Bangalore found that the healthy properties of turmeric were absorbed quickly by the liver, and yet, if added in combination to black pepper, the benefits were absorbed by an astounding 2000 percent more.

During this time, I decided to give a dinner party for my parents' friends, an eclectic and artistic group of people that practice yoga and Qigong, organic farming, and other alternative work. One particular lady, I'll call her Eileen, has tried many diets over the years for health and now basically eschews gluten, dairy, and the like. She watches her blood sugar carefully. I prepared a whole slew of dishes, and since I had just met with Chandran, I brought turmeric root and placed it sliced on the table. One man during the meal complimented me on the carrots. I said, No!

But the best thing was that Eileen called the next day to inquire what had I put in the food! Her blood sugar was way down. I am certain it was the fresh, amazing turmeric root.

JAYABEN'S WALNUT–DATE HALVAH WITH RICOTTA

- 1 pound seedless dates
- ¼ cup sugar
- 2 tablespoons ghee
- ¼ pound walnuts, chopped
- 1 teaspoon cardamom powder
- ½ cup dried coconut, shredded
- ½ cup ricotta cheese

Chop the dates into small pieces. Heat ghee in a pan and sauté dates over low heat. Once the dates start becoming a little soft, add milk and stir over low heat. Once the date and milk mixture is completely soft, add sugar, ¾ cup of the chopped nuts, and the cardamom powder and mix it till it starts to loosen from the sides of the pan. Then turn off the flame and stir it for a little while. Add coconut. When slightly cooled, spread in an 8-inch × 8-inch pan that has been pre-oiled with ghee. Let cool and cut into 1-inch squares.

JAYABEN'S TURMERIC PICKLE

At the home of Chandran and Jayaben, the root was simply julienned and tossed with salt and lemon juice. Here is a more spiced recipe that can keep for some time.

- 2 cups turmeric, grated
- 2 teaspoons mustard powder
- 2 teaspoons methi (fenugreek)
- 2 tablespoons cayenne pepper
- 1 teaspoon salt or to taste
- ½ teaspoon sugar
- ½ cup fresh lemon juice
- ¼ cup oil
- ½ teaspoon black pepper

Peel the turmeric with a vegetable peeler and grate it. You can also use a food processor. Heat some oil and let it cool a bit. Mix in the mustard and methi powder. Do not use hot oil as it will give a bitter taste to the mustard. Add the other spices to the grated turmeric, and put it in an air tight bottle or jar. Add the lemon juice and remaining oil, and mix well. You can later add more oil, or more lemon juice or vinegar as needed. Let this pickle marinate for 2–3 days before serving.

SPROUTED MUNG BEAN FRY *(MATKI CHI USAL)*

This is incredibly chewy and healthy, good with millet cakes and buttermilk lassi. *Matki Chi Usal* is a famous Maharashtrian dish. It's usually eaten for breakfast. Mung beans (or matki beans) are high in protein.

- 2½ cups mung bean sprouts, soaked
- 3 large red onions, finely chopped
- 3 green chilies, finely chopped
- 8–10 curry leaves
- 3 tablespoons oil
- 2 teaspoons coriander powder
- 2 teaspoons amchoor (dried mango powder)
- 2 teaspoons garam masala
- 1 teaspoon mustard seeds
- 1 teaspoon red chili powder
- 1 teaspoon turmeric powder
- Salt to taste
- Fresh coriander for garnish

Soak the beans overnight or for at least 8 hours. Strain the soaked beans and place in a clean cheesecloth. Tie the cloth tightly around the beans. Leave in a warm spot. The humidity of the beans inside the tied cloth allows the beans to sprout.

In a deep pan, heat oil. Add the mustard seeds, curry leaves, and green chilies and allow to frizzle. Stir for a minute and add the chopped onions. Stir until the onions turn golden brown. This will take 10 minutes.

Add the mung bean sprouts and stir evenly. Add turmeric, red chili, coriander, amchoor, and salt. Cover with a lid and allow it to cook on medium-low for 10 minutes. Remove the lid and add the garam masala.

Garnish with fresh coriander.

MILLET ROTIS

Millet is extremely healthy, high in protein, and as more and more people seem to be gluten-intolerant, it is a good choice. It contains a bounty of beneficial nutrients: it is nearly 15 percent protein, contains high amounts of fiber, B-complex vitamins (including niacin, thiamin, and riboflavin), the essential amino acid methionine, lecithin, and some vitamin E. It is particularly high in the minerals iron, magnesium, phosphorous, and potassium.

- 2 cups bajra atta (millet flour)
- 1 teaspoon salt
- Warm water
- ½ cup ghee

Put the millet flour and salt in a large, deep mixing bowl. Make a hole in the center.

Pour a very small amount of warm water into this hole and start to pull the flour into it, adding it slowly. Keep mixing till the flour and water just start to gather. Don't add too much water. The dough is done when it is mixed and soft, like the skin on your arm. Once the flour and water is mixed well, start to knead and continue till you have a smooth, medium-firm dough. When the dough is done, cover with a cloth and keep aside for 20 minutes. Now heat a griddle on a medium flame.

While the griddle is heating, divide the dough into equal-sized portions and roll them between your palms, into smooth balls.

Lightly flour a board with some millet flour. Take one ball and press it flat. Now use a rolling pin, roll it into a circular shape, about 6 inches in diameter and approximately ¼–⅓ inch in thickness. When done, pick this circle up from the rolling board and put it on to the hot griddle. After 30 seconds flip and add a bit of ghee on the edges. Flip again in 30 seconds and drizzle oil on this surface, too. The bajra roti is done when both sides are golden brown.

SPICED LASSI

You may be familiar with the classic mango lassi. This one is savory and spicy.

- 4 glasses of buttermilk or yogurt thinned with water
- 1 green chili, cut into rounds
- 1-inch piece of ginger, grated
- 2 tablespoons lemon juice
- 1 teaspoon salt
- 1 tablespoon oil
- 1 teaspoon mustard seeds
- 4 curry leaves
- 1 tablespoon cilantro, chopped
- ¼ teaspoon red chili powder

Mix the first five ingredients together. Prepare a tadka by heating oil and adding mustard seeds and curry leaves when it is hot. After sputtering, pour into glass of yogurt or buttermilk. Serve cold, sprinkled with a few chopped cilantro leaves and a dusting of red chili.

Chaat Rooms and Comfort Zones

There is no comfort on the street

TIME AND TIME again, in almost every home, families would wax eloquent on the splendors of Indian street food and how lacking America is in this department.

I remember an Iranian friend whose mother came to stay but ended up leaving after a few months. When I asked him why, he said she felt closed up in the house all the time, that no one came out on the streets and talked, and that she felt alone and isolated. It is true that in other countries there is more street life, and thus, more street food.

V and I would go to Washington DC sometimes and stay out until the late hours, sometimes walking the harbor in Georgetown, which is beautiful and lit with shimmering reflective lights. I'm so hungry, he would say, isn't there anything we can get? Unfortunately, no. Absolutely nothing. There are a few late-night restaurants, offering heavy diner food or even a bistro where everyone comes in at 3:00 AM and tends to eat eggs Benedict and fries, but there are no simple kiosks selling a nibble, a sweet, or a tea.

Most Americans are familiar with Indian food from restaurants— butter chicken, tandoori, Chicken Tikka—but few are familiar with the delights of Indian street food.

Chaat is the word used to describe any type of street food in India, especially famous in New Delhi, originating from the Hindi word meaning "to taste." These are usually scrumptious nibbles meant to carry you over in the hours between meals. Chaat can even mean "lick," due to the fact that the treats are often served on banana leaves and one is tempted to lick every last bit. The variety is astounding, and often due to the large non-meating population in India, vegetarian. One popular variety is Papri Chaat, a nice jumble of textures—potatoes, dried noodles, cilantro, chickpeas, onions, tomatoes—tossed last minute with various spicy chutneys and papri (crisp fried rice kernels, like Rice Krispies), and then a sprinkle of the spice mix blend called chaat masala. They are kind of a salad and nibble at the same time, but the textures and flavors pop like fireworks in your mouth.

Chaats can be made with almost anything crispy: fried bits of chickpeas, puffed rice, peanuts, potato tikka (mashed and spiced potato cakes), fresh ginger, mung bean sprouts, or spicy toasted lentils. Chaat masala usually includes amchoor, the tangy powder made from green mangoes, but it must always include kala namak, a black salt that carries a pleasant whiff of sulfur.

These are not the best of times for V and me as the rigors and demands of life start to hit hard. I am very busy with writing, teaching, and my children; he is consumed with school, still, trying to overload on twenty-four credits and transfer to his dream school, the Wharton School of business. In India, when he tried to go to IIT like all math-oriented Indian students, he studied hard; and then there was a time, he says, when he simply dropped off, staying in his room by himself, doing nothing, not going to classes, not eating. To me, it sounded like depression. Call it that if you like, he says. His body has shrink marks on his hips and shoulders from rapid weight loss. I probably lost thirty pounds, he says, his body now delicate and thin. So on some level, the achievement of Wharton would put him back in the running, he thinks. It would reinstate him, prove to the world that he is worthy.

In the beginning of our affair he spent entire weeks at my place. I didn't know how to tell him to go home. He would help me out, filing receipts and doing general office work, or chopping and mixing guacamole, which he lived on. Sometimes he was anxious and other times he would dance around, singing plaintive Hindi lyrics and shaking to Bhangra music, the heavily percussioned songs popularly from Punjab. I have one such picture of him—he is holding a carton of mango juice, his face blurred in joy as he dances. It is funny how random snapshots, taken in an impulse, convey so much meaning in retrospect. They capture an arbitrary moment, which then becomes a significant peak memory. That picture signifies a time of peace, laughter, and joy. But now, tired and pinched by overwork, we would argue. I think the weight of the future finally hit us. I had not been out on a simple date in a year, where a man would take me to a restaurant, share a bottle of wine, perhaps buy me roses. V's severe vegetarianism meant we could go to only certain places—two, to be exact, and they were mainly fast food. We would share a dish, because I was mindful that he largely lived off the grace of his sister's kindness, since he was not allowed to work with his visa, except for occasional in-school tutoring. He drank no wine. The very imbalance of our expectations—my needs and his—were clashing brutally. I grew tired of living the life of a frugal student. I tried to explain it to him: I felt like I was a cake, baked, iced, sitting on a table, and that he was a pile of flour, butter, and sugar. I started to feel life slipping by, speeding by actually, the days as markers towards my imminent old age. I grew tired of cooking meals for him from my lessons. These days our menus were chaat, or maggi, the instant noodles of India.

We lived on maggi and guacamole. It was during this time that things completely broke down, arguments lasting all night, endless phone calls.

If I tried to shut off the phone, he would come over. We were quite frankly codependent and addicted to each other. It felt relentless, yet it felt worse to be without him. I started to become unhealthy, heavier, my hair started falling out.

I WAS LEARNING to make chaat during this time from the husband of a woman named Serena. A Punjabi, she had called me, and we had discussed various options. It turned out that Serena wanted to teach me the same things I had already learned from Ujala—chole, saag, all the North Indian specialties. I was sure she was accomplished, but at this point I needed something different.

How about chaat? I asked her.

Chaat? She acted almost amused. That is a snack, she said.

Yes, I know.

My husband is the chaat man. He makes it every weekend.

And thus, I arrived, with a small camera and my trusty large index cards, a gel-point pen and expectations of salty, savory crunchiness.

I am in the kitchen with Dr. Rohit Singh.

Essentially, he says, this is my favorite hobby. Besides golf. This comment sends him into a huge wave of laughter. Serena hovers nearby, tea in hand, also cackling. He is a serious addict of golf, she says. Their laughter makes me laugh, it is so raucous. And their spicy and unique chai is delicious—strong on the cardamom.

Every weekend we have some kind of chaat. I work all week long so I don't like to deal with this.

He laughs. This is her day off.

They are an older couple, in their fifties, with two teenage daughters whose music from back bedrooms can be heard. They distinctly stay away.

So we need some potatoes, he says. Sita boiled these earlier for me. Apparently, their daughter Sita is the sous chef.

He continues, I've been a gastroenterologist for many years. And I can tell you. This is healthy food. Though a bit spicy. If you have acid reflux, walk out the door! More hearty laughter.

Does your husband like this type of food? I know some Americans do not, he says, as we cut up cold potatoes.

So here comes the moment of the great divide. I can feel it coming. I know I will be examined differently after I make my statement, pitied on some level, or maybe secretly they will be curious or jealous, this woman of the free life. Or this woman of no life, either one. And if they knew the reality, that I have a boyfriend much younger from their culture, what would they think?

I am not married, I say.

Oh, I see.

Oh, so you know of Chandigarh? he says.

Oh, yes, I have friends from there.

Really? He finds that fascinating. He doesn't ask their names. I wonder why.

We continue to chop, now moving on to tomatoes and onions.

Some, they add onions, and some they don't, he says. You see, some Brahmins don't eat onions and garlic. Too rajasic. Do you know rajasic, sattvic, this stuff?

Kind of, I say.

What I know is this: Practically all the Indians I have cooked with have mentioned these things, these Ayurvedic rules. So I have researched and ask questions when in doubt: Basically there are three categories of food, which also happen to refer to types of personality as well. They are sattvic, rajasic, and tamasic.

The ideal of these is sattvic, which is so mild and uplifting as to be considered the ideal food for seers and holy men. It is simple, easy to digest, and has high nutritional value because it is cooked by using minimal heat and modest processing. Another thing: Indians seem to devalue leftovers, unlike Americans. They actually consider it unhealthy to eat food past a day, especially if they are seeking to eat a sattvic diet—which should be taken fresh or immediately after it is prepared.

Nuts, vegetables, dairy, beans, grains and nuts, and many herbs are sattvic. Warm spices like ginger, turmeric, coriander, cardamom, cinnamon, and aniseed are excellent for a sattvic diet. But the ultimate, most sattvic food is cow's milk. That is why you rarely will meet a vegan Indian, most Indian vegetarians tend to be lacto-vegetarians due to the great esteem they uphold for dairy. Vegans believe cows are abused for their milk, yet Indian compassionate vegetarians do not, though they would certainly never kill a cow. Indeed, dairy (as in paneer) is their most venerable protein source, used in everything from appetizers to main courses to desserts to drinks. A milk "walla" in India will sell cow's milk, as well as goat or water buffalo.

Also, rarely would you find a raw food enthusiast in the midst of Indian vegetarians because that diet strongly contrasts with the Ayurvedic concepts of digestion. Digestion, and how it is done in your individual body, is of utmost importance. The key is to develop a pure and strengthening energy called Ojas. A bad diet and bad digestion cause negative energy called Ama, and thus disease. Most people cannot handle a pure raw diet—the work involved simply exhausts their digestive system. A person with strong digestion can handle some raw foods, such as salad or raita, the popular yogurt salad, in moderation, but a faulty digestion needs lightly cooked foods. I have heard eating raw food with a poor digestion is like burning green wood in a fire, thus ultimately futile.

On the other hand, we have rajasic food, which just sounds racier, doesn't it? This is the kind of food we have in restaurants, rich in flavor but heavy to digest. Oftentimes in restaurants it is over spiced and has too much butter or oil. Cooked right, rajasic food is rich in nutrients, heavy on salt and sugar, and takes a longer period to digest than sattvic food. It calls for extended sleeping hours and is sexually stimulating. A rajasic type of diet makes one aggressive and energetic. According to Ayurveda this energy can be beneficial if used wisely; it can lead a person towards prosperity, power, and prestige. A person living on a rajasic diet has love for life and a lust for life. They are focused on exploring life beyond physical pleasures.

Tamasic food is the worst category of food and should be avoided at all costs. Dry, unnatural, overcooked, stale, decaying, and processed food make up the tamasic diet. Tamasic foods consume a large amount of energy while being digested. Refined food—be it cereals, oils or hydrogenated butter, stimulant beverages like tea, coffee, and soft drinks, fast and ready-to-cook food, canned or frozen food, precooked and warmed food items like burgers, pizzas, pastries, and chocolates, as well as intoxicants like tobacco and alcohol are examples of tamasic food.

So, yes, Rohit, I know of these concepts.

He laughs again, a great laugh, rolling like thunder in the room.

We are now mixing herbs to make a cilantro chutney. Most of these chaat dishes are not unusual, mention their name to any Indian and they will probably tell you, Oh, that is my favorite or My mother really makes a good version of that. I suppose you could say it is Indian comfort food. We don't really have that kind of thing in the U.S., strangely enough. Oh, we have snacks—endless amounts of fried this and that, chips, sweets, candy, donuts, but do we have actual recipes for favorite snacks, besides Rice Krispies Treats?

By the time we are done, in addition to the chaat, Rohit has made two chutneys—a simmered tamarind chutney with dates, and the infamous spicy emerald green sauce cilantro chutney that started my love of Indian food many years back. He takes the cooked potato, chickpeas, tomato, onion, and chopped cilantro, tosses them with a nice dose of the chutneys plus yogurt, sprinkles his own blend of chaat masala and a generous tossing of Indian crunchies. This salad/snack is at once soft and sweet, sour and spicy, crunchy and tender—unbelievable.

So, THEREFORE, WE have a snack, a chaat, called Bhel Puri, which is not tamasic but actually sattvic! It is also incredibly fun to make. I brought it to my writer's group the other day. We loved adding things to it, customizing the spices and accompaniments.

One could stage a chaat party with a group of friends. Assemble a table with bowls of toppings, a few homemade chutneys, and your homemade chaat masala. Everyone can mix their own specific blend. Start with a refreshing lassi drink, which you can spike with rum. You can have cups of tomato dal soup with dollops of cilantro crème fraîche, and freshly baked samosas. Finish with rosewater noodle pudding and chai tea. This is a menu that provides casual, exotic fun, plus it can be prepared ahead so you can relax with your guests.

On the chaat table, you will need to have bowls of chickpeas, chopped tomatoes, cilantro, cold cooked red potato, and Rice Krispies. Serve several types of chutneys, such as a tamarind-date or cilantro-mint, and thinned yogurt. If you have an Indian store nearby you can buy the chutneys, crunchy sev and rice crispy chaat mix, and masala, though making them yourself will really make the meal shine. You can also pick up some divali candles at the store, to place on the table for some sparkle.

Rohit, Serena, and I crunch away at his Bhel Puri. I can teach you Pani Puri as well, he says. Or other good snacks. Serena does a lovely Aloo Tikka.

Yes, she says, with a pea sauce, very nice.

We make plans to meet again.

I BRING HOME the Bhel Puri and eat it in the afternoon with some chai I made from Serena's recipe. I have learned that V will be moving an hour and a half away to McIntire, the business school of the University of Virginia, and I am ready to move on, not emotionally in any way, but my age and station in life make me long for the quiet comfortable togetherness I saw in Rohit and Serena.

Married twenty-nine years, he says proudly. I was her least favorite suitor, too!

They pull out the album, faded by time, almost a picture book from another era, a time of royalty and dreams.

Serena is lovely in the pictures.

You will think it was an arranged marriage, yes, I know. In a sense it was. And I know it is hard for you Westerners to get it. But I always say, I get best of both worlds!

He literally shakes and laughs all over.

They have a very ceremonious Ganesh altar, a beautiful Ganesh statue they brought over covered with jewels. There are sprinkles of turmeric around him, and flowers, a banana.

Rohit, when he laughs, reminds me of Ganesh.

You see, he says, I fell in love with this one head over shoes the day I am seeing her. Completely upside down. So when I see she liked suitors better, I talk to her father, I say, Well, let us say I make an offer he can't refuse, like The Godfather.

Serena laughs. I wonder, doesn't the woman pay a dowry?

But he doesn't bring it up.

I am too polite to ask.

This is Indian comfort food, I say.

Oh no, says Rohit. That is something different. It would have to be Khichdi.

Khichdi?

I have heard of this. This is what V's sister made for him once when he was sick. I asked for the recipe. Oh, there is no recipe, it is nothing special. It is baby food.

Khichdi is a sort of mix of lentil and rice with seasoning. Very good, very nourishing.

It is fed to babies for their first food, says Serena.

It was brought to our house, in pots, when my mother died, says Rohit. It is comfort food and mourning food.

It is easy, we can show you, one two three.

Yes. Sometimes we serve it with Kadhi. You know Kadhi?

Yes, of course.

Kadhi: the yogurt stew that Sara taught me, swimming with pakora fritters. Ah, comforting.

Though I have to say, my all time favorite Indian comfort food is Palak Paneer.

I crave it continuously. I made it yesterday, squeezing my own paneer, blending fresh organic spinach, and I must say, after so many versions and attempts, it really hits the mark.

Come on, let's make some Khichdi.

We do, the kitchen fills with warm spicy steam and we eat it in little bowls with yogurt.

Comforting enough for you? asks Rohit.

COMFORT, IS THAT what I seek?

Tell that to my heart when I've told myself a thousand times to move on, and when we've had fight after fight, and when we've cried night after night in each other's arms; for the fatality of it all, the pure mortality of it. Tell that to my heart, which takes the phone calls that come, endlessly; and opens the door, incense wafting, candles glowing, to my tall, young wolf-boy/man who runs inside like he'll never get enough of me.

Tell me, as I leave their warm home with only their borrowed comfort on the passenger seat: Khichdi and Bhel Puri, my heart an empty vessel with wind blowing through.

Yes, temporarily there is comfort in his brown arms smelling of asafetida and warm cumin, there is comfort in his large oval eyes with their brown water deepness, in his fatherly advice and tales. But the true comfort never really exists. Everything comes and goes. These days I don't have many expectations, beyond the sensuality of his small boned back lying in my white sheets. That, and maybe Khichdi.

SERENA'S KHICHDI

* 1 cup basmati rice
* 1 cup toor dal
* ½ cup green beans, sliced
* ½ carrot, grated
* ½ red onion, well chopped
* 1 teaspoon garam masala
* ½ teaspoon turmeric powder
* 1 teaspoon salt
* ½ teaspoon mustard seeds
* ½ teaspoon cumin seeds
* 2 tablespoons ghee

Wash rice and dal five times in water. Soak dal and rice in water to cover. Heat ghee in pan and add mustard seeds and cumin seeds and let sizzle. Add vegetables and cook over medium-high heat. Add ½ cup water and cover, lower to medium-low and allow to simmer till soft. Add more water if necessary. When they are soft and cooked, add garam masala and drained rice mix. Add 3 cups of water. Place in rice cooker or simply cook over medium for 20 minutes until soft and mushy. Serve with a dollop of ghee and yogurt.

SERENA AND ROHIT'S BHEL PURI

A fun appetizer for a dinner party. Serve with small spoons in martini glasses.

- 1 cup Bhel Puri mix, which should include puffed rice, crispy noodle pieces, and small chunks of crisp puri—if you don't have this, you can just use Rice Krispies and crushed instant ramen
- 1 onion, finely chopped
- 1 tomato, chopped
- ½ cucumber, chopped
- ½ cup boiled and chopped potatoes
- ½ cup chickpeas
- ½ mango, chopped (optional)
- 2 tablespoons coriander leaves, chopped
- 1 teaspoon chaat masala
- 1 teaspoon chopped green chili
- Yogurt (stir with a fork to ensure it is very smooth)
- Coriander chutney
- Tamarind chutney

To serve: Toss first 9 ingredients. Drizzle with yogurt and chutneys to taste. Eat immediately while still crisp.

ROHIT'S CORIANDER-MINT CHUTNEY

- 2 cups coriander leaves
- ½ cup mint leaves
- 4 green chilies
- 1 tablespoon lemon juice
- 1 tablespoon tamarind sauce
- ¼ cup yogurt
- 1 teaspoon sugar
- Salt to taste

Mix in a blender until smooth. Add a bit of water if necessary—should be consistency of light pancake batter.

ROHIT'S TAMARIND CHUTNEY

- ¾ cup tamarind juice from a golf-sized ball (see page 221)
- ½ cup seedless dates, chopped
- ½ cup sugar + 1-inch chunk of jaggery
- ½ teaspoon red chili powder
- ¼ teaspoon salt
- 1½ cups water

In a pan add the tamarind pulp, juice, sugar and jaggery, and salt. Add water. Bring them to boil and cook for 10 minutes. If it becomes too thick, add a bit more water. Should be consistency of pancake batter and will become like ketchup when cooled. Cool the mixture and blend it well.

QUICK PALAK PANEER

There are times when I absolutely crave this and must have it ASAP. So, this is my method. Because this is my daily healthy version, I don't use cream, just yogurt.

- ¾ of a store-bought paneer block, cut into chunks (I like Nanak)
- 1 bag of washed spinach
- 1 red onion, chopped
- 1 green chili, chopped
- 2 garlic cloves
- 1-inch piece of ginger, chopped
- 2 teaspoons coriander
- 1 teaspoon cumin powder
- ½ teaspoon red chili powder
- ¼ cup plain yogurt
- ½ cup water
- Salt

Cook onions, garlic, chilies, and ginger in oil. When softened, add spinach and spices. Cook until spinach softens down, about 5 minutes. Place all in a blender with yogurt and water. Blend well and return to pan. Bring up to heat and let cook down, about 5 minutes. Add paneer and let it warm through and puff up a bit. Taste for salt.

Radha and Tamarind Tales

Man is a lonely island

ROHIT, MISHTI, UJALA, Sara, Meena, Suchita, all of them have touched my lives.

And then there is V, who came on the side, like an order of Papad, the crispy cracker of chickpea flour; not something I asked for, but wholly hard to give up.

They have changed my life irreparably. My house is now the spicy one, the one you enter into a prevailing mist of ginger, mustard seeds, and cumin. You will find spirals of chilies in the corners of my house. Ganesh beams proudly from my altar, with incense and candles burning around him, a banana sometimes, or a cookie. I was seeking, I have always been seeking—for many things—love, vocation, God, meaning. Have I found these?

I found love in the most unexpected way, and my friends told me I was crazy.

It will never last, they said.

I was irresponsible, some said.

What are you hoping to get?

I can't believe you would give everything up for sex, said some.

Was it sex?

Certainly. What impulse is not somehow speeded up, tempered, boiled by the incessant desire to touch the one we desire. It is our most human need. Would you be able to pull away from the largest avalanche of desire your heart and body have ever known? Would you walk away from such a primal, stop-you-in-your-shoes basic human want? Have you had that in your life, even once? Most people I talk to say, I don't know if I have ever been in love. They swish the concept around their heads. They think so. Not sure.

Well, people, let me tell you: there is nothing pretty about real love.

To compare real love with the calm yet bloodless let-me-think-about-it affair is like seeing the difference between a common cold and Typhoid fever.

One affects your system, yet with a few remedies you can adjust, drive the car, or go to work. A few sniffles, yes. Tired and cranky, for sure. But Typhoid comes and make no mistake, you are knocked to the ground. The same with love. Does it make sense, is it a good choice, is it sensible, is it feasible? No, no, no, no. None of the above. But I, the person who always found it elusive, the one always in control, find it inconceivable how useless I am now to fight, to pull back. How removed from my head all of this is, how my heart seems to be limitless in its capacity to adjust in this particular romance.

I am completely attached to V, as if a tree mushroom growing on a log, just there, unable to move, a part of him somehow. Infuriatingly there.

AND IN MY search of God, the true spiritual sense of what that means, the incomprehensible, what have I learned?

That I am still seeking.

That I am looking inward not outward.

Where religion ends, spirituality begins: The disconnect with religions occurs when original teachings become rigid and outdated, losing the reason of the original spiritual leader. Thus, the dogma becomes incestuous, harboring a belief that their way is the only path to salvation. Thus it can be that religions separate us from one another, spawning violent wars, hatred and division in the world.

Spirituality is the original essence of every religion; it is the common denominator that unites all faiths and beliefs in the one human aspiration towards mergence with our divine source. Spirituality focuses our attention on the divine residing in our hearts, revealing an indefinable essence, called God for lack of a better word, in the light of proximity and intimacy. Being within us, God is thus a part of us. All that a spiritual person seeks is oneness with God or Self, urging us to focus the mind inwards and to approach this inner presence with love. The best method to observe this part of ourselves is to slow down, observe. Be it in meditation or prayer, or even quiet watchfulness. While cooking. While making love. Feeling the moment entirely. Feeling your connection to all that is.

It is summer and V and his sister are leaving to go to North Carolina on a pilgrimage to see their Babaji, their master of Radhasoamis. I will be going to Maine like I do every year. Last year, I went with my family and with V, and yet this year, I don't bring it up. The college transfer decisions have come in and he did not get into his beloved Wharton, so he is crushed. But instead, he will attend the prestigious McIntire School at the University of Virginia. Now, I thought his transfer would herald in a period where we could maybe find separation, in an easier way, through distance. I thought that life itself would take care of all the problems and pain this relationship poses. I guess I was naive.

A relationship between two people of such differing ages—twenty-five years, in our case—forces you to face mortality. Like Benjamin

Button, I had the sobering experience of aging before my beloved as he seems to grow forward. Not only physically, but psychologically as well. As V prepares to go outward into the world, I am savoring my position, resting. The inevitability of aging feels like a sad waiting game. A wrinkle here, a pocket of cellulite there, a gray hair, these are harbingers of deeper separation. Here I am, focusing on the spiritual side of life, when the animal physicality refuses to shut up. There is also resentment, because fighting the avalanche of aging is a loser's game, and tiring. And, somehow, undignified. On some level, I want to age without the backdrop of a younger man to offset the contrast.

When I was a young girl, very young, my favorite book was *Chéri*, by Colette: "The tragicomedy of the boy who will not grow up and the woman who cannot stay young" it says on the book flap. There is one particular scene that always stayed in my thoughts, freshly remembered years later, that I find haunting. In the story, Léa is a beautiful courtesan of a "certain age" who finds herself in a relationship with Chéri, the son of her best friend. The affair lasts for years, and then one day he must marry a society girl. Léa feigns indifference, but is stricken with despair and goes off to live in the South of France. Chéri does his duty but is deeply depressed. Finally years later he can stand no more and goes to seek the company of Léa. In a final scene, he sees her once again:

> A woman was writing at a small table, facing away from him. Chéri was able to distinguish a broad back and the padded cushion of a fat neck beneath a thick gray vigorous hair, cut short like his mother's. "So I was right, she's not alone. But who on earth can this good woman be?"
>
> "And at the same time, write down your masseur's address for me, Léa, and his name. You know what I'm like about names . . ."

These words came from a woman dressed in black, also seated, and Chéri felt a preliminary tremor of expectation running through him: "Then . . . where is Léa?"

The gray-haired lady turned around and Chéri received the full impact of her blue eyes.

"Oh, good heavens, Child—it's you."

He went forward as if in a dream, and kissed an outstretched hand.

"Monsieur Frederic Peloux—Princess Cheniaguine."

"Is he your . . . ?" Queried the lady in black, referring to him with as much freedom as if he had been a deaf-mute.

Once again the great peal of girlish laughter rang out and Chéri sought for the source of this laugh here, there, and everywhere—anywhere but in the throat of the gray-haired woman.

Desperate, broken, and disillusioned, Chéri leaves and finally in the end of the book, kills himself with a pearl-handled gun. Melodramatic, yes, but the book does pinpoint the bittersweet and tragic edge such a relationship bears. One is constantly forced to peer into the abyss of mortality. In another type of relationship, the usual one with similar ages, the couple can pass through time together, but in mine—one is left to witness, aghast, the advances of time.

How odd it is that my favorite book when I was twelve was the story of a woman and a man twenty-five years apart, and then years later, I actually live it out? Was I so impressed as to seek it out or was I privy on some level to my destiny? One can only muse.

And so, going to Maine alone becomes a silent division somehow. I am quietly letting go, as is he. We must. Maine would be too bonding.

Last year in Maine was the first time he saw the ocean. I told him it was the bay, not the ocean, but he was spellbound by the ceaseless blue slash of water displayed from every window, a cool horizontal peace. We went to the rocky shore, threw stones, seaweed; sat. He said he wanted to make love there in front of it. I said it was too rocky. He insisted. On the last night, I was sleeping but he woke me, saying we had to go. He was always a thoroughly pushy type. It felt impossible not to bow to his will eventually, as he simply never gave up. But I went back to sleep and he was angry. The next day, he was sullen and we left Maine.

We left the kids for another week with my parents, and drove home alone. At some point in the long drive he reminded me that I had crushed his dream. Come on, I said.

Then, we were hungry: I suggested we take the next exit, Westport. I knew this town somewhat because my ex-husband's family was from here. It was just turning dusk. Take this road and go straight, I told him. He drove through winding turns of the town, past statuesque houses of wealth, pockets of forest meandering throughout the glossy town, a bit too nouveau for real elegance, a bit tinselly, but with that Connecticut plainness. Where are we going? he kept asking, when suddenly we turned at a corner of pine trees, and there—the blue ocean stretched out in front, solemn, cold as slate.

We sat by a fading bonfire someone had left on the sand. We walked. He couldn't get over it. Again and again he would shake his head, put out his arms, say, Wow. He played in the waves with his pants rolled up. We retreated to the car, sandy. And then, as darkness came, I consummated my promise.

Afterwards, whenever he was feeling sentimental, he'd say: Thank you for the ocean.

This year, though, we go our separate ways.

When I come back from Maine this year, he is already in his new apartment in Charlottesville.

I keep cooking.

RADHA AND I had emailed back and forth, not quite connecting because I thought she was a man (someone told me this name could be both) and she doesn't have a place to teach. She had insisted on my house, so I felt nervous. But finally I pop up again and say I could come over, and we resolve the whole thing. She is, however, from the start, rather abrupt and curt. Demanding. She wants to teach four hours, I ask for one and a half or two hours. She says it better be two if it is worth her time. I feel rather offended, but think I will still go.

She lives right by the community college V had attended and one more stab of pain comes my way. I have begun to feel as if a series of these exists around me, reminders of how I didn't fit in his life, on the physical level. I didn't feel comfortable going to his school with him, walking around, a soccer mom on the arm of a sophomore. I would feel belittled, no doubt, or thought of as a harsh cougar on the prowl. V would insist that he had no issues with this, but I still felt unsettled, bad. I felt he was bluffing. I knew it would be an embarrassment.

As I drive into Radha's neighborhood, I see occasional Indians walking the streets and I know I have entered one of the areas—usually off Route 7—where they live in enclaves, close to the E-tech companies that sprawl down that corridor. I drive to a very unkempt townhouse, the grass completely seedy and yellowing. A smiling small woman in a salwar kameez greets me, brings me in, and says, I usually live down here, pointing to the basement, but the family I live with is out of town, so we can use up here.

She brings me up to the main rooms and the kitchen. The house is remarkably cluttered with bric-a-brac, plastic flowers, holiday decorations, product boxes, everyday junk. The kitchen also, every counter completely covered in mail, containers, spices, spoons, nothing seemingly has a tidy spot. I can see devotional, guru pictures here and there. Briefly I wonder if she is Radhasoami. I don't ask.

She makes a lovely chai, rummaging for spices, using cardamom husks in the tea—I save them for tea, she said—and slices of ginger, and then she proceeded to teach me. Unlike the others, Radha is very abrupt, charmingly so: Chop some tomato, please, she will say, while Ujala insisted that she do everything herself and I watch.

We are making Sambar, and Eggplant in Coconut-Peanut Curry. We begin by roasting peanuts in a pan—and, as she first lights the pan, she very sweetly puts her hands together and prays silently for one second. I watch and say nothing, but of course, she may as well have thrown a match on a giant pile of newspapers, for the smoldering of my natural spiritual curiosity has been kindled. We then stand on the porch and roll the peanuts in our hands, blowing away the skin. It is time consuming, yet peaceful. She insists that Indian peanuts are better, sweeter, and I try one and yes, it is true. We grind these with roasted chilies, coriander seeds, and methi, and finally add the paste to coconut milk. Fried eggplant is the next ingredient. (This is wrong type, she scolds, next time buy round Indian eggplant. I had asked an Indian woman at the store which one, and she said these were. Probably she is from wrong part of India, said Radha.) And so we have a rich and creamy curry, warm and delicious. As she makes Sambar we talk. I discover that she has a master, as she puts it (a guru), and that it is not Radhasoami, but Sahaj Marg, a group located in Chennai. She tells me that she started meditating on her own, and she tells me, in a very quiet voice:

One day I was meditating, in the dark, with my eyes closed, and a bright light came on. I opened my eyes, thinking I had left the light on and I saw my master walk right by me. I knew him. Then I realized he had come to me.

Then apparently she found this master who appeared to her, Sri Ram Chandra. I tell her how I am seeking, that I am thoroughly intrigued and interested in Raj Yoga (yoga of the mind) and have been reading about it for years, meditating on my own. She insists I come to her meeting.

We talk further and I learn that Radha has left her children and is separated from her husband, and has come here alone. She lives in this house, of a family who also follows the master, and I believe she cooks for them in return. She is in school and dreams of becoming a lawyer and sending for her children. I now understand her harsh demanding way with her time—most of the other women that I worked with had husbands. She is on her own. In a way, I am the most like Radha of all of them: both of us single moms, trying tooth and nail to make it in the world.

I leave that day with my two boxes still steaming with her food. I am grateful.

That night I learn of her "path." According to their website:

Sahaj Marg is a form of Raja Yoga, or yoga of the mind. The goal of the practice is God realization, with the supposition that the true Self is one with God, and it is only our individual complexities that block our conscious experience of the divine. Because the divine is infinite and without attributes, the object of the meditation cannot have any name or form, so we are given the most subtle and pure thought to meditate upon—divine light in the heart. We do not visualize the light but only suppose that it is present. As other thoughts arise, we gently divert the mind back to the heart and wait patiently for this divine presence to manifest.

We know that the heart is the center of the physical system, where the blood is purified. In keeping with the Indian Vedic tradition, Sahaj Marg teaches that the heart is also the center of the spiritual system, where our inner condition is purified. Therefore, the focus of our meditation is on the heart, specifically the place where the heart beats.

It is a lovely concept. But, I research more and learn that there are some concerns it is a cult. In fact, many of these Raja Yoga branches and "paths" have cult-like qualities that raise red flags in our culture, but within the history of the Indian culture they do not concern—the paths of Sai Baba, Radhasoami (Sant Mat), Krishna—because of their heritage. Historically, the Indian educational system worked under the guru style—one would select a guru and move to his ashram to further his study. It mimicked family patterning, and blind obeisance was expected. In our more independent culture, we find this questionable. Still, the Indian methods of Raja Yoga, deep mediation that leads to an experience of God, entice me. I tell her I will go with her to meet her master the following week.

Radha responds back in her typically acerbic fashion: I told you my master is in Chennai. You can come to my meeting, however.

I eat her Sambar that night, very spicy.

In the morning I awake at 4:00 AM and start meditating. It is very difficult, my mind scurries around, anxious, worries about me and V; and worse, I am now getting hot flashes on a regular basis.

I am deeply in need of rest.

RADHA'S SAMBAR

Sambar is basically a spicy vegetable and dal stew, deepened by the hue of tamarind juice. It is delectable with dosas, idlis, or steamed rice.

- 3 carrots, cut into 3-inch pieces
- 3 green serrano chilies
- 6 okra pods, ends cut off, cut into four pieces
- 1 zucchini, cut into 1-inch chunks
- 1½ cups toor dal
- 4 cups water
- 1½ teaspoons turmeric powder
- 1 die-sized piece of jaggery, or 1½ teaspoons brown sugar
- 1 golf ball–sized piece of tamarind, softened into juice (see page 221)
- 3 tablespoons sambar powder
- ½ teaspoon salt

Place everything in a pressure cooker and cook for four whistles, let cool. Or cook in a pot, covered, for 45 minutes. Add tamarind juice, salt, and sambar powder. Let cook on low for 5 minutes to accommodate flavors. Taste for salt (commercially prepared sambar mixtures may have salt).

RADHA'S EGGPLANT IN PEANUT-COCONUT CURRY

* 3 tablespoons oil
* 5 red chilies (to taste; I found this amount was not too spicy, but you might not agree)
* ½ teaspoon methi (fenugreek) seeds
* 1 clove garlic
* 5 teaspoons cumin seeds
* ½ cup coriander seeds
* ½ cup raw white sesame seeds
* 15 small Indian eggplants or 5 Italian eggplants
* ½ cup Indian peanuts in the shell
* 1 cup coconut milk
* ¾ cup fresh or frozen coconut, unsweetened
* ½ cup tamarind pulp (see page 221)
* 1-inch cube of jaggery, or 2 tablespoons brown sugar
* 1½ teaspoons salt
* ½ cup cilantro, chopped

Wash and cut eggplant into "bunches" as Radha referred to them—sever lengthwise into long pieces without cutting off the stem, much like a bunch of bananas. This allows the sauce to permeate. Fry eggplant in oil, covered, for about 20 minutes, flipping occasionally, until soft and cooked.

Toast peanuts in a pan for 10 minutes until golden brown. Place on a baking sheet to cool, placing outside if the weather is cool. When cooled completely, rub and blow away skins until clean. Meanwhile, toast chili, methi, garlic, coriander seeds, cumin seeds, and sesame seeds in a pan with one tablespoon oil until browned and seasoned, about 10 minutes. Place everything—peanuts and spice mix—in food processor and blend, adding a bit of water to facilitate. Add the coconut milk. Add this mixture to cooked eggplant. Add coconut. Add salt, tamarind juice, and jaggery. Stir and simmer for 5 minutes. Top with cilantro.

Peace and Pakoras

At the altar of all that is

I HAVE COME BACK to Ujala or maybe I never left. All the Indian women of this year—all, unequivocally all—have been amazing cooks. Intuitive, sensitive, completely aware of their ingredients, respectful of the process in a religious sense, offering thanks or blessings to deities beforehand. The act of cooking, though they also have busy schedules, is not disrespected. It is thought of as showing homage but it is also considered necessary for family and individual health. A great respect for this act emanates from all the families.

Ujala and I meet less often now, sometimes not for weeks. Our schedules have clashed here and there, and Ujala has traveled—Niagara Falls, New York City. She is returning home in a few months. You will visit me in New Delhi, I hope, she says, and I would very much like to.

Our last meeting has been changed to a Saturday instead of our usual Wednesday. I come to the door, and I don't know why but I hesitate, I sense somehow she is not expecting me, but no matter.

I ring the door and I hear a scurrying. After a bit of a delay, she comes to the door, graciously greets me, and I see that her daughter is in full sari, her son-in-law well-dressed, all have the traditional mark of holy ash and red powder, kumkum, on their foreheads. Uh oh.

Hi, Nani, come in please.

I can tell I have intruded at a special time and I feel really bad. I enter but it's awkward; I'm not sure if I should leave, or stay, but I take off my shoes and go to the kitchen in the middle of the room, where I can see large bowls of food already prepared.

It is more than obvious that she forgot I was coming.

Today is Durga Puja, and we are going to the temple, she says.

Oh no, I say, I am sorry. I can go.

No, Nani, please stay.

She tells me the history of Durga, the myth, but actually I can't always understand Ujala's accent. Her daughter comes in and explains it in pieces. They have me sit down and they show me family pictures. They tell me this festival marks the end of a nine-day fasting called Navratri and today is solely for the Mother Goddess—Maa Durga. The name Durga means "indestructible" in Sanskrit, and she is the personification of "Shakti," or female energy. She shows me a small picture— Durga is riding a lion, and carrying weapons in her ten arms. She is very beautiful.

We haven't eaten yet, we are about to offer a puja to Durga, to give her thanks and food, and then we will eat.

I again offer to leave but they insist I stay. I ask them to please start.

Her daughter and son-in-law move to a center of the room, next to the kitchen. Ujala kindly stays in the kitchen and starts chopping vegetables. Remember that everything is in one large room in this apartment. Ujala is cooking. I stop her. Please, Ujala, go with them.

Even though she had forgotten I was coming she, graciously enough, plans to still break her plans to be with me. Ujala is such a kind lady.

She protests a bit but then she goes, leaving me in the kitchen.

EVEN THOUGH V moved to his school—and he wouldn't even say what day he was leaving because he didn't want to say goodbye formally—he still calls me. He still came over last week. We talk four, five times a day. I thought it would end. I have talked to him endlessly about what we will do. In fact, we have spent our entire two years together talking of this: What we will do. But what we always end up doing is nothing.

I try not talking to him for a week, but eventually I break down.

It was my forty-eighth birthday last week. He came to see me, and he gave me a present. A card that seemed vague and unromantic. He is afraid to promise anything.

I think I am ready to move on. The time has come for a new direction.

A time to own my own space.

UJALA COMES OVER to the kitchen and grabs my arm.

Come on, she says.

She pulls me into their circle of family. The husband is wrapping the daughter's wrists with a red string that is called "moli." I learn there are lots of reasons for this string, such as to remember to always use your right hand in puja, and to bind yourself into the service of God by invoking God and ask for His/Her blessings that only good deeds may be done with your hand. The string also represents the bond between Atma (soul) and Paramatma (God); it protects its wearer from evil sprits or habits; and finally, as the string is tied around your hand, you pray that your life will similarly revolve around God. But Ujala also tells me that during puja one must always wear new clothes, and since you can't always have new clothes, the moli signifies them.

I watch as the son-in-law lovingly ties it around the wrist of Ujala. And then he pulls me forward.

I feel extremely moved. Tears are prickling in my nose and eyes and I fight them with every bit of my will. I don't want to look like an idiot. He ties the string around three times. We all hold hands. He starts to chant, and everyone follows. The son-in-law now goes to the altar—the same carved metal one I have secretly been looking at for so long, soaking in its mystery, longing to know its secrets—and kneels in front. In his hands is a metal plate holding a tiny container of lit oil, ghee I believe. The family is mouthing the mantras and I am silently praying.

Inside the altar, I see the tiny figure of Ganesh.

Oh Ganesh! What a journey it has been.

The son-in-law brings the fire over and we whisk it towards ourselves, cleansing ourselves.

They ring the bell.

And then Ujala brings over a tray of puris with chole—the first thing that I ever made with her.

They put this in front of the fire and the altar. And then, after praying some more, they sit down and break their fast.

I feel almost as if I have left my body, so wonderful is the feeling. Then Ujala starts to teach me the food of the day. I try and beg out of it, but it is too late. They will go to temple later, she says.

She chops the vegetables slowly.

When I leave their house, the usual food under my arms, I feel buoyant, transformed. I will cook with Ujala until she leaves for India in December, but I crossed a line. I felt included, finally. After this whole journey of being an outsider, I was somehow let in briefly.

It is the same with V and me. What started as a love affair, a curiosity, a thing of lust and fascination, has grown to something so much larger than we ever knew. We have become family, on some level. It is beyond just the bedroom, or the heart. It feels like we belong to each other in the blood.

Divali is in a few weeks. I will start cleaning my house thoroughly as is the custom. This year, I can cook all the right foods, maybe I will even do a puja myself.

THE PHONE RINGS and I see it is V.

I ignore it.

Again.

I ignore it.

Once again, and I wonder if I can keep ignoring it or will I break down. When will it ever stop? I am driving along the countryside of Virginia, the sun is falling behind the hills:

I answer the phone.

He sings my voice, as he likes to do: Naaaaneeeee.

Another day on this earth, we are bound.

WHEN I WAS married to my ex-husband for ten years, I was happily entrenched in the customs of a Jewish household. We would attend massive Passover seders each year, long rituals with food meant to celebrate the Israelite exodus from Egypt, along with traditional foods, wines, songs, and prayers. It is a fun family night, endless and joyous, and it was a highlight each year.

One thing I loved: at the end of the hours-long ritual, everyone would hold up glasses of the famously over-sweet Manishevitz wine, and toast, "Next year in Israel!"

So, in that spirit I hold up a cup of chai, and vow, "Next year in India!"

In my office, looking at my Ganesh statue, I ask myself, Did Sri Ganesh remove any obstacles? And I would have to say, Yes. They were called doors. They were opened, in many ways—physically, spiritually, emotionally—clearing the way for a new path, one of truth and connection.

And good food. So onward to a new year.

In the meantime, I cook.

And love.

UJALA'S BHATURE

A famous accompaniment to Chole.

- 1 cup maida (white flour)
- ½ teaspoon baking soda
- 1 teaspoon baking powder
- ½ teaspoon salt
- ¼ cup yogurt (for fermentation)
- ½ cup of water mixed with 1 tablespoon canola oil
- 1 teaspoon canola oil

Place maida in a bowl, whisk in dry ingredients. Make a well in the center, add yogurt, and start crumbling together, while squeezing with your hands to mix. It will be very crumbly. Now add oil and water mixture and knead well until the mix is soft and bouncy—press the skin on your stomach, it should feel like that, soft. Pour oil over the mix and knead for a good solid 2 minutes. Cover with a damp cloth and let this sit for fermentation 2–4 hours.

For frying: Heat 2 cups oil in a pan to 375°F. Oil is ready when a small piece of the dough dropped in will immediately rise and start sizzling. If it sinks, wait a few more minutes.

Put a small bowl of oil next to the stove along with a rolling surface and rolling pin. Start by putting some oil on your hands, the rolling pin, and the rolling surface. Pull a small hunk of dough the size of a walnut, roll very quickly into a thin circle, 4 inches in diameter. Place in hot oil with your hand, and push down with spatula as it browns very quickly. Flip after 1 minute and brown other side. Drain on a tea towel.

Serve warm with chole.

UJALA'S POORI

Ujala made these fried puffs of bread frequently. They were sumptuous and not hard to make. Puris are famous for picnics and lunch boxes—the oil keeps them from drying out like parathas or rotis do.

- 2 cups atta flour (whole wheat flour)
- ¼ teaspoon salt
- Ajwain seeds (Also called carom seeds, available in Indian markets, they really add flavor)

Place flour, salt, and seeds in a bowl, mix well, then make a well and add water, mixing and kneading, until "tight," as Ujala said. Put aside for 5 minutes. Knead again and smooth out the bumps. Sprinkle with a little oil. Knead quite well until soft. Let sit for 10 minutes.

For frying: Heat 2 cups oil in a pan until 375°F. Oil is ready when a small piece of dough dropped in will immediately rise and start sizzling. If it sinks, wait a few more minutes.

Place some oil on rolling pin and rolling area. Pinch a walnut-sized piece of dough and dip lightly in oil. Roll to a thin circle 4 inches in diameter. Place in oil and press down with spatula—this will make it start to puff up. When light golden in color and completely puffed up, flip over for 30 seconds, then pull out of oil and drain on a waiting cloth-covered plate.

Getting Started:
The Basics of Indian Cooking

*I*N ORDER TO prepare proper Indian food that will knock your socks off, I suggest the following: change your thinking radically. Stop thinking about cooking as a chore and start embracing it as a ritual, a gift that you are giving your family and friends. Don't worry about short cuts and saving time, but instead try and buy food with the greatest natural energy, from farmers' markets if possible. Respect your tools and keep them handy and basic. Turn your kitchen into a hearth, not a showpiece. Let it be a little greasy, a little used-looking. Enjoy the lingering smell of spices in your air, like incense. Appreciate the Indian idea of *andaza*—cooking with your senses. Use your hands as much as possible, imparting your love and energy into the food.

Now, with a changed attitude, you are ready to make the best vegetarian food you will ever have. One more thing: In my recipes I have used the amount of salt and oil the women taught me. It may seem excessive at times. It is your choice; you can cut back on both if you wish, it won't affect the dish too much. But you must use enough oil for proper searing and cooking.

The most valuable thing to know is the concept of *andaza*—cooking with your senses and instincts, not with measurements and timing. I have given you measurements and timing on all the recipes, but I have also given you very easy visual clues—how it should smell, how it should look, how it should feel. These are far more important. These will teach you much more than just cooking: they will take you out of your head and into your heart and body. Each ingredient, each stove, each pan has its own personality and you will learn how long each step will take. You have to sense it, to know it. But I suggest you first cook according to my timing! The second time you cook, ignore these and take a chance—use your eyes, ears, and nose to guide you. You will then start to use this more in life, to trust your senses and your instincts.

You ARE NOW ready to get started . . .

Here are some key elements of Indian cooking that are not too complicated, but essential:

1. *Bhuna*: Hindi for "fry in oil." Almost all Indian food starts with a base. Many recipes in this book start with the Punjabi base of ground or sliced onions, tomatoes, ginger, and garlic. There are variations, of course. Some Brahmins, for example, disdain onions and garlic as too stimulating, or rajasic; Southern Indians use items such as nuts and coconut as a base, and these are also taught in this book. But in general these four ingredients—onions, tomatoes, ginger, and garlic—are the starting point of a "gravy."

Learning to cook down the base slowly and then adding the spices so they "roast" is key to a well-developed flavor. What destroys a dish is not properly cooking the paste or gravy down, which will result in a dish that tastes raw and crunchy or watery. The key is to cook it slowly until oil appears around the edges. This is the key moment to add the masala or spices for roasting. Adding the spices too quickly will burn them.

2. *Tadka (or Baghar)*: These terms mean roasting whole spices in oil. The tadka is the essential last spicing of many dishes. After the dish is

prepared, there is a secondary garnish, if you will, of oil-cooked spices that further pumps up the dish: It not only visually rounds out the flavors perfectly, it also adds a dosage of flavorful ghee. (I noticed they do this in Brazil with feijoada. After cooking the stew with onions and garlic, they brown some in oil in the last minute to stir in.) When the tadka is done, you've essentially layered the onion-garlic flavor in two ways. Tadka is usually prepared in a round metal sauce pan the size of a measuring cup. In desperation, I sometimes use a stainless steel 1 cup measurer.

3. *Masala*: "Masala" means spice in Hindi and of course it is the vital ingredient in Indian cooking, which uses more spices than any other cuisine in the world. It is vital that you obtain fresh spices and roast them before grinding. It will make a big difference. Many Indians I worked with used store-bought spice blends for various dishes—they are not bad and you may wish to do so. On the other hand, if you make your own, the flavor will explode. I have listed what types to buy to get started.

TOOLS
I would like you to consider buying a simple pressure cooker. Indian women are able to eat their delicious homemade food every day because of this wonderful tool. Call it the healthy microwave. It can make dal, chickpeas, or potatoes in ten minutes. (Potatoes are considered the Indian fast food, incidentally, and I was told to always keep a few cooked cold ones in the fridge for a quick fry.)

Another item to have is a slow cooker, which can be used for stews you want to leave cooking all day and have ready for dinner. And, of course, have a small food processor, a blender, or a mortar and pestle. I also suggest a coffee/spice grinder in order to blend your own spices. Indian cooking is amazingly economical. These items really help.

Additional tools I find helpful are:

1. *Spice (or Masala) Dabba*: A round tray with a lid that holds eight small bowls for spices and a few spoons. This will allow you to have all the spices handy and you won't have to keep opening jar after jar, which makes the kitchen instantly chaotic. I keep in my dabba—sea salt, turmeric, ground coriander, ground cumin, garam masala, whole cumin seeds, whole mustard seeds, and red chili powder. You could use a series of baby food jars without lids in a shoebox, if you want. But try and find a method, because it does really help.

2. *Indian rolling pin*: Unlike the American versions, the Indian rolling pin is very skinny and really helps roll out chapathis and puris, etc. They are wooden and cheap. Buy one.

3. *Kadhai*: A small cast-iron wok for frying. I recommend it, but a small stainless steel pan is also fine.

4. *Tawa*: A small cast-iron flat pan, about 6 inches wide, for cooking breads. A flat pancake pan is fine. Many Indians use Teflon. There are some concerns about the health hazards of Teflon when heated to high temperatures, so I prefer cast iron.

INGREDIENTS

You will need to go to an Indian store or order online. I am not going to Americanize everything with substitutes, because it won't taste good and you won't benefit from all the excellent Ayurvedic properties. Obviously, there is no "curry powder," which is an anglicized concoction invented by the British colonists. There are, however, masala powders—mixtures invented for various dishes. It is preferable to make your own, though you can purchase quality ones. To be honest, most women I cooked with bought these mixtures and used them quite frequently. I decided to seek out the recipes for my own blends and have found them to be fresher. I did try different premade brands and found some of them quite good, and have included their names. Here is a basic list of what I would suggest to start you out. You will spend very little and receive a lot. Do NOT buy from an American store; you will spend a huge amount for a tiny bit of spice, and it will probably be quite old.

SPICES (MASALA)

- Turmeric

- Coriander Seeds (I recommend you roast and grind your own powder)

- Cumin Seeds (ditto)

- Black Cumin Seeds (shah jeera)

- Red Chilies, whole

- Red Chili Powder

- Amchoor (ground sour mango powder)

- Black Mustard Seeds

- Cinnamon Sticks

- Bay Leaves

- Black Peppercorns

- Cardamom Seeds

* Asafetida (hing, a resin from a tree, with a distinctive oniony pungency)

* Ajwain Seeds (when roasted they develop an aroma similar to caraway)

* Black Salt

SPICE BLENDS

* Chaat Masala (or buy Badshah or Everest)

* Chole Masala (or buy Badshah)

* Paneer Masala (or buy Badshah)

* Garam Masala (same)

* Kitchen King Masala (This is used in Punjabi food. I can't find the spice ingredients, so this one you would have to buy.)

* Tandoori Seasoning (this is vegetarian)

PANTRY ITEMS

* Chapathi Flour

* Pooji Flour (farina)

* Chickpea Flour (besan)

* Dried Block of Tamarind

* Urad Dal

* Toor Dal

IN ADDITION

- Fresh Ginger

- Limes

- Cilantro

- Yogurt (plain)

- Garlic (fresh)

- Red Onions (Indians prefer these as they have less water)

- Green Serrano Chilies (You may also use jalapeño, but they are less spicy)

This is a basic list; it will last you a long time and bring you endless delicious meals that will have your family and friends raving. You will feel immense pride and energy from cooking like this.

To start I would suggest you spend one Sunday afternoon shopping and getting things ready. Buy the ingredients and fill your spice dabba. Cook some ghee and keep it by the stove.

Make your own masala blends. Here are a few recipes for general dishes I use in the book. You can buy them premade, as I said. However, at least try and make the garam masala as it really makes a difference.

GARAM MASALA

Roast in a pan over medium heat until dark brown and aromatic, about 10 minutes:

- 1 tablespoon black pepper
- 2 tablespoons cumin seeds
- 2 tablespoons coriander seeds
- 1 teaspoon fennel seeds
- 1 teaspoon cloves
- 1 tablespoon cardamom, whole
- 1 small cinnamon stick, broken up
- 1 teaspoon black jeera (cumin)
- 2 bay leaves

When ready, let cool for a bit, just until the heat is dissipated. Grind in a coffee grinder until a fine powder. Keep in a tight jar.

CHOLE MASALA

- 1 tablespoon coriander seeds
- 2 tablespoons cumin seeds
- ²/₃ teaspoons black cardamom seeds
- ¹/₃ teaspoons cardamom seeds
- 1²/₃ teaspoons black peppercorns
- 2–3 dried red chilies
- ¹/₃ teaspoon whole cloves
- A pinch of ground ginger
- A pinch of mace
- A pinch of nutmeg
- ¹/₃ teaspoon ground cinnamon
- ¹/₃ teaspoon amchoor (ground mango powder)

Dry roast the seeds, peppercorns, chilies, and cloves in a large frying pan over low heat until they begin to brown. Transfer to an electric coffee grinder with the ground spices and grind to a fine powder.

Makes about ¹/₃ cup. The recipe can be increased if you want to make a larger quantity.

CHAAT MASALA

- 1 tablespoon cumin seeds
- 1 teaspoon fennel seeds
- 1–2 dried red chilies
- 1 tablespoon coriander seeds
- ½ teaspoon black peppercorns
- 1 tablespoon amchoor (ground mango powder)
- 1 tablespoon black salt
- 1 teaspoon red chili powder
- 1 pinch asafetida powder
- ½ teaspoon sea salt

Dry roast the spices separately in a heated frying pan. Add to a grinder and blend.

HOMEMADE GHEE

Do not under any circumstances substitute margarine. In fact, throw that stuff away—it is absolutely horrible for you and tastes awful. If you must, use a pure, organic vegetable oil.

- 1 pound pure salted butter, preferably organic

Cook butter over medium-low heat. It will crackle for 10 minutes as the water is cooked away. When it is clarified and separated and a nice golden hue, strain it into a jar through a cheesecloth, or just pour carefully, leaving the solids in the pan. Keeps indefinitely and you can keep it on the counter.

Preparing ghee and garam masala will add an unmistakable identity to your food. You can buy these premade in the Indian store, but I really think you will find that the homemade versions add immeasurable flavor.

MASTER RECIPE FOR PANEER

I am absolutely crazy for Indian cheese, or paneer. When you first taste it, you might think it seems very bland, much a like a block of cottage cheese, and in fact it is quite similar. However, it is mild and seems to soak up whatever sauce it is cooked in. It is used in many recipes, fried as fritters, used in sandwiches, and stuffed in breads. You can buy paneer from the Indian market, but it will have no taste in comparison to homemade. If you have had it in an Indian restaurant, it was probably rather hard and tasteless—this recipe will give you the authentic favor of paneer. One other thing: Some Indians like to have fresh paneer for breakfast, sprinkled with a bit of red chili, lemon juice, and grated cucumber, which is very nice.

- ½ gallon container of milk, preferably organic
- ¼ cup vinegar or lemon juice
- Pinch of salt
- A new white cotton T-shirt cut into a large square, or a large piece of cheesecloth, moistened with water and placed in a colander

Heat milk in pan and bring to a boil, then turn down to medium-high and let it cook for a few minutes. Add salt and then lemon juice or vinegar. Stir slowly with a wooden spoon, and watch: it will go from white to separated large curds in a yellowy clear fluid. When it is quite separated, remove to sink and pour into a colander lined with cheesecloth or T-shirt. Rinse a few times with cold water to remove acids, and then tie up by four corners and let this hang (over the faucet) for about 15 minutes.

When this is done, press down on the colander, twist the top a few times and place a small plate with a heavy object on top (a large can of beans or a mortar). Let rest for half an hour in the colander.

Done! Remove cloth and place paneer on plate in refrigerator until ready to use.

TAMARIND PULP

- 1 walnut-sized piece of tamarind (or whatever the recipe calls for)
- ½ cup hot water

Let soak for 20 minutes and then start squeezing with your hands. Add more warm water if it gets too thick. When very dark and thick—texture of ketchup—strain and keep aside.

Acknowledgments

HERE ARE SO many people to thank concerning this book that I don't know where to begin, but I might as well start at the beginning: I want to thank my parents, Ann and John McCarty, who have provided endless—and I mean endless—love and support to this woman who is struggling in the world. This project took a huge amount of time and love, and they helped me in many, many ways—financially, emotionally, and were always ready to take their grandchildren if I needed time. I don't know that many people who have their loving patience and I am truly grateful. I also want to thank my father, Mark Power, for his considerable love and respect for my work, which is a big deal to me. He—and my stepfather, John McCarty—have shown me through example the honorability of being a devoted artist. I respect their unwavering devotion to their own work, as well, as great examples of commitment. Many thanks to PRW group and especially Cathy B. for much support.

I thank my children for their endless joy and love, and for sampling my cooking experiments. My dear friends who always tell me how wonderful my work is—I love you all: Natalie, Tracey, Lisa, Briget, and Cathy.

I want to thank V.A., whom I write about in this book. His devotion, love, and kindness are exemplary. I've never met anyone like him and I doubt I ever will.

My amazing agent Wendy Sherman has stood by me in many years of writing with endless support, advice, wisdom, and friendship. She is savvy and yet very, very kind. Thank you.

My editor on this book, Laura Mazer, what a delight you have been. I loved your warmth, charm, and brilliance. I am also amazed by the skillful editing of Trish Hoard, whose eagle eye really shaped this book. Katherine Little I must thank as well for also patiently helping lift this project off the ground.

Lastly, I want to thank a group of women—strangers—who came into my life and taught me Indian cooking. I thank them for being so brave to come to a new country and start anew. I thank them for loving their culture and food so much that they would care to teach me the gift of such a thing. And for their trust and yes, love, to allow me to learn, eat, and even worship with them. Such generosity can never be forgotten.

About the Author

NANI POWER IS the author of a memoir and three novels, including the critically acclaimed *Sea of Tears*, and her stories have appeared in numerous literary magazines. She lives in Virginia.